RULERS OF INDIA-
LORD LAWRENCE

Owing to the antiquity and rarity of this book, certain pages are regrettably absent, and readability is compromised due to the blurring of the original text. If you possess any insights regarding the availability of these missing sections, kindly inform us. Your assistance is crucial in ensuring the completion of this significant work for the benefit of future generations.

RULERS OF INDIA-
LORD LAWRENCE

OR, A RETURN FROM INDIA,
A NOVEL, IN A SERIES OF LETTERS

EDITOR

WILLIAM WILSON HUNTER

GYAN

Published by

Gyan Publishing House
5, Ansari Road
Daryaganj, New Delhi-110002
Phone: 011-47034999, 9811692060
E-mail: books@gyanbooks.com

Distribution Network
gyanbooks.com
India, USA, Canada, UK, Australia

ISBN: 978-93-7133-608-6 (PB)

First Published, 1892

2nd Impression 2025

Printed at: Gyan Press, Delhi.

RULERS OF INDIA-LORD LAWRENCE
Editor: WILLIAM WILSON HUNTER

Rulers of India

EDITED BY

SIR WILLIAM WILSON HUNTER, K.C.S.I., C.I.E.

M.A. (OXFORD); LL.D. (CAMBRIDGE)

LORD LAWRENCE

HENRY FROWDE, M.A.
PUBLISHER TO THE UNIVERSITY OF OXFORD
LONDON, EDINBURGH
NEW YORK AND TORONTO

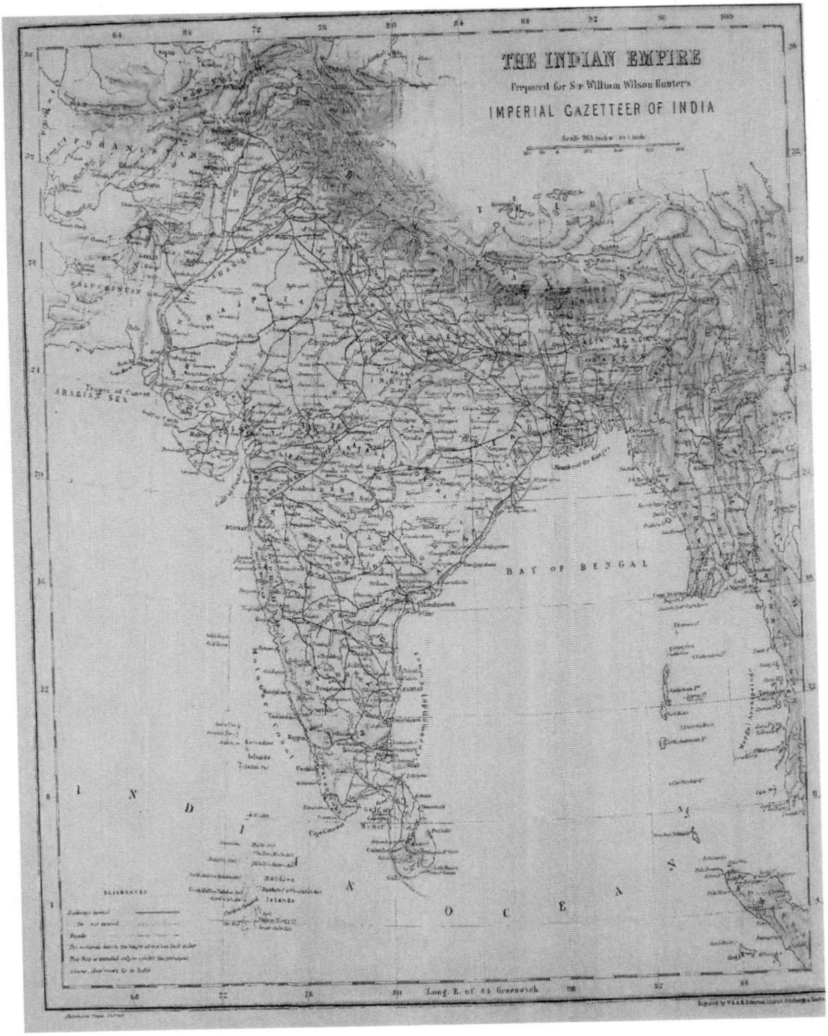
THE INDIAN EMPIRE
Prepared for Sir William Wilson Hunter's
IMPERIAL GAZETTEER OF INDIA
ARABIAN SEA
BAY OF BENGAL
Long. E. of Greenwich

RULERS OF INDIA

Lord Lawrence

AND THE RECONSTRUCTION OF INDIA UNDER THE CROWN

SIR CHARLES AITCHISON, K.C.S.I., M.A., LL.D.

FORMERLY LIEUTENANT-GOVERNOR OF THE PUNJAB

THIRD THOUSAND

Oxford

AT THE CLARENDON PRESS: 1894

PREFACE

THE life and achievements of Lord Lawrence have been already written, both in large and small. There is the exhaustive work of Bosworth Smith; there are sketches by Captain Trotter, Robert Cust, Dr. George Smith, and others; and there is the vignette by Sir Richard Temple in the 'Men of Action' series. The circumstances and events of his time too have been recorded by many pens. It would seem, therefore, as if there was no room for another monograph. But the series of the 'Rulers of India,' without a notice of the man who both saved India and ruled it, would be so incomplete that, as there may still be variety of treatment, even if nothing new be said, I have been induced to try.

For the events of Lord Lawrence's life and times I have freely used existing biographies (especially Bosworth Smith's), the ordinary histories, Blue Books, Administration Reports, and official papers kindly put at my disposal. For some local touches I am indebted to the Settlement Reports of the Delhi, Karnál, Gurgáon, and Rohtak Districts. The Settlement Reports of the Districts of our Indian Empire are mines of information—antiquarian, historical, scientific, statistical and general—too little known in this country.

The information available from the above sources has been supplemented by my own personal recollection. I served under Sir John Lawrence's orders, in the rank and file of the Civil Service in the Punjab, through the year of the Mutiny and afterwards till he left the province. When he returned to India as Viceroy, I was his Under Secretary for Foreign Affairs for more than a year, and for a short time his Foreign Secretary. And being called on, toward the end of my service, to govern the Punjab, I found there still the impress of his master hand, weakened indeed by time and change, but not obliterated.

It may be thought that in the chapter on Afghán affairs I have not observed due proportion. There is ground for this. Sir John Lawrence's policy and action have been so much misunderstood that I have thought it best to give a plain narrative of facts with quotations from documents. It is essential to know not only what Sir John Lawrence said and did, but the time at which and the circumstances under which he said and did it. If my own conclusions be thought to be those of a disciple, the facts are there, and the reader will judge for himself.

C. U. AITCHISON.

30th April, 1892.

CONTENTS

NOTE

The orthography of proper names follows the system adopted by the Indian Government for the *Imperial Gazetteer of India*. That system, while adhering to the popular spelling of very well-known places, such as Punjab, Poona, Deccan, &c., employs in all other cases the vowels with the following uniform sounds :—

a, as in woman : *á*, as in father : *i*, as in kin : *í*, as in intrígue : *o*, as in cold : *u*, as in bull : *ú*, as in rúral.

LORD LAWRENCE

CHAPTER I

INTRODUCTORY

THE close of Lord Elgin's brief Viceroyalty of twenty months[1] was overclouded by political troubles on the Punjab frontier.

A colony of fanatical Muhammadans had settled, in the early part of the present century, on the right bank of the Indus, near the Mahában Mountain, and had, for many years during the Sikh rule, kept the country in perpetual unrest. Sayyid Ahmad, the founder of the colony, was a British subject, and his followers were largely recruited by fugitives from justice and discontented men from British territories. Bodies of armed men, sometimes numbering five hundred or six hundred, made their way to his standard. He had organised a regular propaganda, the centre of which was at Patná in Bengal, and had established agencies in different parts of India for the levy of

[1] Assumed office 12th March, 1862; died at Dharmsala 20th November, 1863.

money and the supply of arms. The prayers of pious Mussulmáns followed him. The imperial palace at Delhi, the minor Muhammadan princes and the great cities of Lucknow and Hyderábád supplied him with funds.

Inflamed with fanatical zeal, his avowed object was to wage war, in the name of religion, against all unbelievers in the Muhammadan faith. Bigoted Patháns, from the turbulent tribes of the Pesháwar border, flocked to him in numbers, animated not less by the hope of plunder than by zeal for their creed. For many years his daring inroads, in one of which he captured the city of Pesháwar, kept the Sikh armies on the alert and gave employment to the most active generals of Ranjít Singh. Sayyid Ahmad was slain in battle in 1831.

His death depressed for a time but did not extinguish the colony. Recruited by ever-fresh accessions of bigoted and desperate men, the fanatics contrived to keep the Sikh border in a constant ferment. With the annexation of the Punjab, the British Government inherited these frontier quarrels and the ferocious animosity of the colonists. They had to be chastised in 1853, and again in 1858. On the latter occasion their settlement at Sitána was burned, they were driven from their villages, and engagements were taken from the neighbouring tribes never to permit their return. These engagements, however, were not observed.

In 1862 the colony once more began to give trouble, and in October 1863, a force of six thousand men of all arms, under command of Brigadier-General Sir Neville Chamberlain, moved out against them. A halt in the Ambela Pass, attributed by the enemy to weakness and hesitation to advance, had the effect of uniting the neighbouring tribes against us; and what was intended to be an expedition to chastise a handful of fanatics suddenly developed into a frontier war, in which we found ourselves opposed to a coalition of all the tribes between Pesháwar and the Indus. For two months the British troops lay in the Pass, unable to advance, and subjected to attacks by night and by day. The Punjab was denuded of every available soldier to reinforce the position; and the campaign, which lasted till the close of the year, cost much blood and was the most serious frontier affair in which we had ever been engaged.

Matters were at their worst, calling for the personal intervention of the Commander-in-Chief, Sir Hugh Rose, when Lord Elgin died. It was this frontier war which 'clenched[1] the appointment' of Sir John Lawrence, 'beyond the possibility of doubt,' to be Viceroy and Governor-General in succession to Lord Elgin. Sir John Lawrence had already successfully directed expeditions against the fanatics, and severely chastised them. He had defeated all their efforts to enlist the Amír of Kábul against us, and to effect a hostile coalition of the frontier tribes in the most desperate hour of our fortunes. The treaties which, under the inspiration, and with the help of Sir Herbert

[1] Bosworth Smith, vol. ii. p. 385.

Edwardes, he had concluded with Dost Muhammad Khán, had converted into a faithful ally the man who had been 'by turns the rejected friend, the enforced enemy, the honourable prisoner, the vindictive assailant' of the English in India. 'I have now made an alliance with the British Government,' said the Amír, 'and come what may I will keep it till death.' That promise, made three short months before the revolt of the Sepoy army, was never broken, even when the Punjab was so denuded of European troops as almost to invite an Afghán invasion, and when the priests of Kábul and the Amír's own sons were calling him to bind on his head the green turban of Islám and sweep the English from the plains of India.

In those dark days of 1857, too, when the valleys of the frontier lay defenceless and open to the freebooters from the mountains, Sir John Lawrence had dexterously drawn to his service the marauders of the border. Adventurers from many tribes—Afrídís and Mohmands, Dáúdzais and Yusafzais, even robbers from Boner and zealots from Swát—had answered his call, and had marched, regiment after regiment, to fight our battles on the Ridge at Delhi and on the plains of Hindustán. Lawrence's splendid services to the State, his soldierly qualities, his firmness and energy and fertility of resource in difficulty, his adroitness and penetration in native diplomacy, his straightforward bluntness in meeting Oriental artifices, combined with his knowledge of border politics and his experience of tribal modes of warfare, singled him out as the man best qualified to deal with the serious entanglements into which frontier affairs had drifted. There was no living man whose antecedents gave better or equal assurance of ability to correct the military and diplomatic blundering which had converted a petty expedition into a dangerous war, and had produced a political crisis in which even the fundamental duty of loyalty and allegiance came to be gravely discussed among our Muhammadan subjects.

The war was over some three weeks before Sir John Lawrence arrived in Calcutta. But the cheers which greeted him as he landed showed that the appointment was a popular one, apart from the special circumstances which had 'clenched' it. There were many in England, and in India too, who looked upon this as only a fitting recognition of the unique services which had drawn the eyes of the world upon him and made his name a household word. The Government of Bombay had been already offered to him and declined. It was meet and right that John Lawrence should, in the Queen's name, govern the empire he had done so much to save.

Lord Elgin's messages to India were peace and goodwill, reconstruction and progress. He had, in 1857, seen Calcutta when the English were staggering under the first shock of the Mutiny. He had witnessed the first outburst of mingled surprise and panic and rage and vindictiveness when the Empire seemed to be crumbling to pieces. He had heard the deep and savage cry for vengeance, and had realised the bitterness of the race hatred which the events of 1857 had evoked. The gaping wounds which the Mutiny had inflicted were little more than skinned over when he returned five years later as Viceroy, in 1862. The storm of evil passions had subsided, but the race antipathy was deep. There was a clamour for reconstruction on English lines and English principles. Englishmen were flocking in numbers to the country. Waste lands and tea-cultivation and new enterprises of various kinds were attracting English capital. The rights of the Native population were in some danger of being overborne by the demands of the dominant race under the influence of a prejudiced public opinion. If Lord Elgin had lived out his term of office, his genial disposition, his varied knowledge of men, and his experience in the arts of diplomacy and administration, would have gone far to accomplish the work of reconciliation and secure due consideration to the claims of the Natives. But his short reign left it little more than begun.

Sir John Lawrence's qualifications for the task were of a different but not less effective kind. He had won the gratitude of his countrymen, the devotion of the army, and the admiration of the Natives of India. There was a sentiment in each class to which he could appeal. The task of pacifying the people and healing old wounds he knew to be difficult —more difficult even than the reconquest of India. 'It is a task,' he had once said, 'which the bravest and best may shrink from. It is one in which a great man may break his heart and lose his life, and which, even should he, by God's help, accomplish it, will never be appreciated.' But if any man was likely to bridge over the gulf between the Native and the European, it was Sir John Lawrence, who could speak the Hindustáni language as fluently as English, and who had governed a province in the administration of which the Native had from the first been more closely associated with the European than in any other part of India.

On the other hand, in the work which lay before him as Viceroy Sir John Lawrence had special difficulties of his own to contend with. He returned to India a commoner as he had left it. He was not adorned with the titular rank and dignity which had long hedged round the person of the supreme 'Rulers of India.' He was destitute of those social graces which go far to conciliate opposition and disarm prejudice. He had risen from the ranks of the service. His proposals, therefore, were certain to be canvassed with unusual freedom; and it was almost inevitable that his measures, when not approved of, should be opposed with more than ordinary persistency, even by those who were loyal to him at heart. 'He and I,' wrote one of his colleagues, 'have always been good friends, and all the better that we were on a footing of equality; I am not so sure how this will last when he is superior.'

Mindful, probably, of the bickerings which had impeded Warren Hastings in his administration, and had more than once brought the government of the country to a deadlock, Lord Cornwallis, in writing to Mr. Dundas on the choice of his successor, had given it as his opinion[1] that 'nobody but a person who had never been in the service and who was essentially unconnected with its members, who was of a rank far surpassing his associates in the government, and who had the full support of the Ministry at home, was competent for the office of Governor-General.' For three-quarters of a century these recommendations had, with one single exception, prevailed in the selection of the Governor-General. John Lawrence possessed none of them save the last. By constitution and training, moreover, he was not well suited to work in multiple harness. He made up his own mind quickly, and had the courage of his opinions. Protracted discussions were a weariness to him, seldom producing conviction. 'I am not well fitted by nature to be one of a Triumvirate,' he wrote, when member of the Board of Administration at Lahore.

The romance of Sir John Lawrence's life was the Mutiny year. His Viceroyalty was on the whole peaceful and uneventful. But it was a germinal time, a time in which seeds were sown that brought forth much fruit in later years. It fell to him first, in the work of reconstruction, to give full effect to the Royal Proclamation in which the Queen had expressed her 'earnest desire to stimulate the peaceful industry of India, to promote works of public utility

[1] Marshman's *India*, vol. ii. p. 51.

and improvement, and to administer its government for the benefit of all her subjects resident therein.' His Viceroyalty was a time in which the Native Princes of India were permitted to 'enjoy that prosperity and that social advancement which can only be secured by internal peace and good government'; a time when none of the subjects of Her Majesty, of whatever colour or creed, 'were in anywise favoured, none molested or disquieted, by reason of their religious faith or observances, but all alike enjoyed the equal and impartial protection of the laws'; a time when the Natives of India were 'protected in all rights connected with the land, subject to the equitable demands of the State'; and when 'in framing and administering the law, due regard was paid to the ancient rights, usages and customs of India.'

CHAPTER II

THE DISTRICT OFFICER

THERE was nothing in the boyhood or early life of John Laird Mair Lawrence to give indication of a brilliant future. It was not till the forty-sixth year of his age that the opportunity came to him to show his heroic mould and 'the iron nerve to true occasion true,' though he had before then distinguished himself as an exceptionally able administrator, a man of self-reliance, vigour, and resource, and had risen to an eminence in India not often attained so early in life.

John Lawrence was the eighth child and sixth son in a family of twelve, born to Colonel Alexander Lawrence and his wife Letitia Catherine Knox. Both parents were of families which had for generations been domiciled in Ireland. But the father, a gallant old soldier, who as a lad had volunteered for India and there purchased his commission only after he had twice earned it by gallantry in the field, led the wandering life of his profession; and so it came to pass that the children counted their birthplaces in various parts of the world. John was born on 4th

March 1811, at Richmond in Yorkshire, where his father's regiment, the 19th Foot, happened at the time to be stationed. The mother was a shrewd, thrifty, God-fearing woman, with great administrative qualities, who 'kept the family together' on scanty means. I am afraid, however, that the traditions which make her of the lineage of the great Scotch Reformer through Andrew Knox, Bishop of the Isles and of Raphoe, are mythical. At any rate it is certain that the blood of the Reformer did not flow in her veins[1].

Both parents possessed much character. It was probably from his mother that John Lawrence derived his vein of quiet evangelical religion and unobtrusive Puritanism. But it was the father who stamped the character of his boys. 'I should say,' wrote one of them in after life, 'that on the whole we derived most of our metal from our father.' Colonel Alexander Lawrence gave five sons to India, all of them in their way remarkable men; and two of whom, Henry and John, have built themselves an everlasting name. The life of the stout old father had been an adventurous one. He carried the seams and scars of a hard and honourable but ill-requited service, and all his life endured the buffetings of adverse fortune. He was 'a mine of memories,' and the stirring stories of a chequered life, told at the fireside and in the daily walks, fell on the mind of the boy John like generous seed, awakening in him military ambitions and making him in later life, as his brother Henry said, 'in heart

[1] See Note A.

and action more of a soldier than half the men who wear red coats.'

From his earliest years John had set his heart on being a soldier. 'A soldier I was born,' he exclaimed when the supreme moment came to decide on his future—'A soldier I was born, and a soldier I will be!' The remonstrances of his veteran father and the counsels of his brother Henry were unavailing to change his mind. But the persuasions of his much-loved sister Letitia, with perhaps a thought of his mother and the *res angusta domi*, at last prevailed to turn him from his purpose. He sacrificed his personal ambitions and accepted the 'writership' in the service of the East India Company offered him by Mr. John Huddlestone, who had already provided his elder brothers with cadetships.

Four years (1819–1823) as a day scholar at College Green, Bristol; two years (1823–1825) at his maternal uncle's school, Foyle College, in Londonderry; and two years more (1825–1827) at Wraxall Hall, in North Wilts, with desultory reading in Plutarch's Lives and sundry books of history, constituted his general education before he entered Haileybury and commenced the special preparation for his Indian career. School did little for him. But the glorious associations of Derry seem to have produced an abiding impression on his mind. More than two centuries have passed since Derry made her heroic defence. But the story of her Spartan endurance has never lost its freshness. The blood still warms and the pulse beats quick as one reads in the graphic pages of Macaulay how the great fastness of Protestantism in Ulster, 'betrayed, deserted, disorganised, unprovided with resources, begirt with enemies,' shut her gates in the face of King James and endured the memorable siege of a hundred and five days. Its effect on the young schoolboy was deep and lasting. Long afterwards, in the height of his fame, when he revisited Lahore with the Viceregal mantle on him, Sir John Lawrence told, in a public address, how the blood of the old defenders of Derry warmed within him as he fought in India against fearful odds, and nerved him for his work.

He entered Haileybury in July 1827. There he proved himself a good but not a specially distinguished student, passing out third in the order of merit in May 1829. Accompanied by his sister Honoria, and his brother Henry, he sailed from Portsmouth on 2nd September 1829, and, after a voyage of over five months, during a great part of which he suffered severely from sea-sickness, landed in Calcutta on 9th February 1830. This was an unfortunate time to arrive. The short winter was already over. The heat of summer was beginning and the sickly months of the rainy season were close at hand.

Calcutta was at that time a very unhealthy place, with little resemblance but in outward features to the city of the present day. Cholera was endemic. Drinking water was procurable only from open tanks, exposed to all kinds of pollution. It was carried in the common leather skins used by the water-carriers for miscellaneous purposes, often no doubt to carry water that was putrid and contained the germs of disease. The river was the common receptacle for the half-burned corpses of the Hindus, which floated up and down with the tide, or stuck in the chains of the shipping, giving out the most sickening stench, and affording a loathsome meal to hundreds of carrion crows. The city was practically undrained. The sewage festered and bubbled under the tropical sun in open ditches till removed by scavengers. The place had no attractions for John Lawrence, though it may have suggested to him some sanitary reforms which he carried out in later years. Here, however, he had to remain for ten months to pass examinations in the Hindí and Persian languages before he could be pronounced fully qualified for work up-country. He was ill nearly the whole time. His biographer tells us he was often heard to say that an offer of a hundred pounds a year in England in those days would have taken him straight home.

Towards the end of 1830, he passed his examinations and escaped from the enervating and sickly climate of Calcutta, of which he entertained a hearty dislike to the end of his days. At his own request he was appointed to the Delhi Territory, the cradle and the theatre of his future fame. Here, early in 1831, he began his work as Assistant to the Resident, and served for eight years—four years' apprenticeship as Assistant, two years as Magistrate and Collector of the District of Pánípat, and two years in charge of the District of Gurgáon. During these years he received a thorough training in all departments of the civil administration, and acquired that complete mastery of details without which he never considered a Civil Officer to be fit for his duties. With him there was no royal road to become an efficient Officer—no road at all other than hard work and regular training. An apprenticeship had to be served in these things. His own appetite for work was insatiable. At Pánípat he worked for two years, morning, noon, and night; and to this he attributed his fortune. 'During my charge of the Pánípat District,' he tells us, 'I completed my training as a Civil Officer. It was a hard one, it is true, but one which I had no cause ever to regret. It has facilitated all my subsequent labours, no matter how varied, how onerous. I had become well acquainted with the duties of an administrator both in a large city and in an important agricultural District. I had come in contact with all classes of the people, high and low. I had made acquaintance with most of the criminal classes, and understood their habits of life. I had seen all the different agricultural races of that part of India. I had learned to understand the peculiarities of the tenure of land, the circumstances of Indian agriculture, canal and well-irrigation, as well as the habits, social customs, and leading characteristics of the people. . . . The experience and the credit we gained stood us in good stead in after years.'

No finer field than the Delhi Territory could at that time have been chosen for the development of the special characteristics by which John Lawrence was distinguished. There was scope for independent action and opportunity for the display of individuality of character and temperament which the administration of an ordinary British District did not present. The Delhi Territory came into our possession when the Maráthá confederacy was crushed in the war of 1803. The aged Emperor, Sháh Alam, the same who, eight-and-thirty years before, had ceded the civil government of Bengal to the English Company of Merchants, was now rescued by the armies of his 'faithful servants and sincere well-wishers' from the thraldom of the Maráthás, and restored to his throne under English protection. The puppet King went through the form of conferring on the English the territories they had conquered, and the victors on their part assigned for his support certain Districts on the right bank of the Jumna, and a money allowance equal to more than £120,000 a year. The city of Delhi and the assigned lands were excluded from the operation of the Company's laws and placed under charge of an officer styled the Resident and Chief Commissioner, who collected the revenue and administered justice in the Delhi King's name. The King and Heir Apparent carried with them, outside the royal palace, personal exemption from the ordinary laws, while the precincts of the palace were treated as foreign territory in which the King's authority alone prevailed. Here in the Hall of Audience—round the cornice of which in letters of gold upon a ground of white marble, in the graceful characters of the Persian language, ran the famous lines, 'If there be a Paradise on earth, it is this, it is this'—the King held mimic court. Surrounded with all the paraphernalia of imperial dignity, he received from his protectors the symbols of an allegiance they did not pay, and affected to dispense an authority he no longer possessed.

For more than a quarter of a century the coins of the Company continued to bear the superscription of the Emperor; and the representative of the Governor-General did him obeisance. Everywhere the people of India looked to him as the fountain of honour. No Prince of a Muhammadan House, no Chieftain of ancient lineage in Rájputána, conceived his title to be quite complete till he had obtained the recognition of the Delhi King. In vain our Government discountenanced these pretensions, in vain it substituted the royal effigy of England on its coinage for the imperial superscription, in vain it declined to recognise the validity of titles granted by the Emperor. Do what it might, the Company was unable to clothe itself with the prestige which encircled the imperial throne, and this phantom as it seemed of a vanished power continued to exercise a strange but real fascination over the people of India. To ambitious spirits, brooding over the memories of departed greatness, it was a visible figure ever recalling what had been; ever suggestive of what, by the blessing of Allah, might yet again one day be. To the evil-disposed and disaffected, and to all who were ripe for mischief, it became a focus of intrigue. And, as we shall see, it formed a rallying point for the military revolt which shook the foundations of the English power.

Perhaps things might have been different had Lord Wellesley carried out his original design to remove the King to a distance from Delhi. But this was never done. In fact it was found convenient at first to govern in his name. Authority which seemed to be delegated by him procured more ready acceptance for the government of the foreigner. And when at last the English stood forward in their true position of paramount supremacy, the mischief was already done, and there was no remedy. Lord Dalhousie indeed recommended that, upon the death of Bahádur Sháh, the royal title and prerogatives should cease. The proposal however was opposed by the Court of Directors. They yielded only to the overruling power of the Board of Control; and Dalhousie, in deference to their objections, abstained from using the authority he received. But although the King's grandson was recognised as Heir Apparent, it was only on condition that he should quit the palace at Delhi.

This fate was impending over the ancient House of Timúr, when the Mutiny intervened. John Lawrence well knew the dangerous associations which centered in and round a city that had for generations been the throne of empire. He knew it was the prestige arising from the possession of Delhi that gave to the revolted

Sepoys half their strength and power for mischief. He knew that with the fall of Delhi the cohesion of the Mutiny would dissolve like snow in a thaw. In the dark days of the great military rebellion, it was not till Delhi fell that he began to breathe freely again and felt that the extremity of the crisis had passed.

There was no strong poetic vein in young Lawrence to which the faded glories of the Imperial House could appeal. His character was above all things practical. Yet fond of history as he was, his imagination could hardly fail to be impressed by the ruins of ancient cities covering many square miles of country, whose annals ran back some sixteen centuries to the story of the Mahábhárata. They had seen the rise and fall of many thrones and dominions, Hindu and Pathán and Mughal and Maráthá. But his sympathies were with the peasantry rather than with the Princes; with the village communities, 'the indestructible atoms,' as Elphinstone calls them, which survive all revolutions rather than with the dynasties which succumb. His honest spirit was stirred to indignation by the vice and debauchery that festered within the walls of the palace. His sympathy with the masses was roused by the unpunished crimes of the nobles, the violence of the grandees, the insolence of their retainers, and the oppression of the petty Chiefs, many of whom had palaces of their own in the city, where they came to swell the tawdry pomp of the mimic court. What he saw and learned at Delhi inspired John Lawrence with a strong and abiding conviction of the blessings conferred by British rule on the industrial and agricultural classes, and furnishes the key to the policy he afterwards pursued as Chief Commissioner of the Punjab and as Viceroy of India.

The Delhi Territory was full of refugees from the Native States bordering it on three sides, which had been created by the British Government in pursuance of a policy now long exploded, or carved out by the swords of martial horsemen in the days embalmed in the local annals as the 'Sikh hurly-burly.' When the Maráthás were stripped of their conquests in Upper India, our acquisitions beyond the Jumna were considered as an encumbrance. Most of them were given away in reward for services during the war and in pursuance of the policy of the day which sought to create a belt of dependent States from Karnál to Agra. It was made a condition of these grants that the Chiefs were to settle the country with their own troops and we were to have no concern therewith. And some years later, the petty Sikh Chieftains, over whom our shield was thrown to save them from Ranjít Singh, were maintained in the same rights and authority within their possessions as they enjoyed before they were taken under British protection.

In the course of time and under the gradual development of the British power, the little Sikh Rájás and Sardárs have all sunk to the position of ordinary subjects. Most of the petty States [1] we created have

[1] It was the Chief of one of these States who instigated the murder of the Commissioner of the Delhi Territory and whose

also disappeared. Five of them threw in their lot with the rebel King of Delhi and were consequently extinguished. Three only—Pataudi, Lohâru, and Dujána—remain to this day. But when Lawrence was at Delhi, nearly all of them were still in the full possession of their power, with unlimited opportunities to oppress, untempered by British interference. Their jurisdictions interlaced in the most perplexing way, and every Chieftain levied tolls on traffic according to his fancy. Everything was taxed—the caravan of the merchant and the head-load of the peasant, the rich man's luxuries and the poor man's necessaries—and payment to one Chief gave no exemption from the rapacity of another. No fewer than ten different kinds of rupee were in circulation, which were received into the British treasury at fixed rates of exchange.

The country round Delhi is purely agricultural. Here it was that John Lawrence acquired his experience as a Revenue Officer, and that intimate knowledge of tenures and the economic condition of the peasantry which underlay all his future land policy. In the neighbourhood of the city and in the hills to the south, there is a large population of Gujars, elsewhere a quiet and pastoral people, but in Delhi of evil reputation. In the south of Gurgáon the Meos or Mewátís, believed by some to represent the original

capture was cleverly effected by the energy and detective ability of John Lawrence. The story is graphically told in Bosworth Smith, vol. i. pp. 74–78.

non-Aryan inhabitants of the country, predominate. These are predatory races, thieves and cattle-lifters, a turbulent people, who were ever a thorn in the side of the Muhammadan Government and have given much trouble to ourselves. But three-fourths of the population of the Delhi Territory belong to honest and industrious agricultural tribes. The flower of the peasantry is the Ját. Not a few of the villages can trace their pedigree back for more than a thousand years and, amid all the revolutions of time and changes of dynasties, have preserved written annals of their history from a time when William the Conqueror had not yet landed on the shores of England. The vitality of these village communities is marvellous. 'They are admirably adapted,' wrote John Lawrence, when Collector of Delhi, 'to resist the evil effects of bad seasons, epidemics and other evils incidental to this country. Bound together by the ties of blood connection, and, above all, common interest, like the bundle of sticks . . . they are difficult to break. Drought may wither their crops, famine and disease may depopulate their houses, their fields may be deserted for a time, but when the storm blows over, if any survive, they are certain to return.'

The country is specially liable to drought. Part of it is protected by canals, but the cultivation generally is dependent on the rainfall, which is exceedingly uncertain. When the rain fails everything is lost; the grass and the young crops wither away; the cattle begin to die; the ground becomes hard as iron; not an acre can be ploughed, not a seed can be sown; and when the clouds collect and the rain falls at last, there are no oxen left to draw the plough. Once at least in every ten years, generally oftener, severe scarcity or actual famine may be expected. The official records of the Districts enumerate twelve such years since 1803, and the memory of earlier famines is preserved in the traditions of the people. In the 'Famine of '40' thousands died of disease and want; even rich men died of starvation; food was not to be purchased for money. The 'Famine of '17[1]' lives in the mouths of the people and in the village songs—'grain sold at the price of pistachio nuts and wheat at the price of raisins;'—'the trader lived and the Ját died; the carts remained useless, for the oxen were dead; and the bride went to her husband's house without the due formalities.' Two terrible famines occurred, one in 1833 and another in 1837, when John Lawrence was serving in the Delhi Territory. That of 1833 was intense and forms an epoch from which old men fix the date of events. Even the wolves and jackals, from feeding on human flesh, became more ferocious and lost their fear of man. Lawrence in describing it as an eye-witness says, 'As early as the end of April, there was not a blade of grass to be seen for miles, and the surrounding plains were covered with the carcases of the cattle that had died from starvation.'

[1] The year 1840 of the Hindu Calendar = 1783 A.D.: and the year 1917 of the Hindu Calendar = 1860 A.D. Just so we say 'The Rebellion of '45.'

In those days the Company's government of the Delhi Territory was supposed to be patriarchal. But the revenue administration was thoroughly vicious and hardly less oppressive than in the worst of the Native States. The assessment of the land tax was fixed at a ruinous rate. The demand was never paid in full. Balances were always accruing. When the revenue of a village was overdue, horse and foot were quartered on the inhabitants till everything was squeezed out of all who could pay. One hundred and thirty-six horsemen were retained in Pánípat for the collection of the revenue, while twenty-two were considered sufficient for the duties of police! No wonder the revenue settlements broke down. An estate was considered fairly lucky if it escaped re-settlement every five years. Almost all the assessments which Lawrence made were large reductions on the previous demand. Even then, his settlements sometimes broke down too, from the extreme destitution of the peasantry and their want of cattle, implements of husbandry, and even the necessaries of life. 'In going over the records,' he wrote, 'one is often amazed at the excessive assessments which have been realised.' Naturally he had ever after a horror of over-assessment. Light taxation of the land was to his mind the panacea for foreign rule in India. 'Do not be hard on the Zamíndárs,' were his instructions to Charles Raikes, his Assistant in Pánípat; 'Government revenue of course must be paid, but do not be hard: "the calf gets the milk which is left in the cow."' 'Mind you assess low,' he wrote to George Christian, when entering on his settlement work in Jálandhar; 'if you don't, I shall be your enemy for life, and indeed, what is worse, you will be your own. Let nothing tempt you to assess high.' A contented and prosperous peasantry he looked upon as the bulwark of the empire. Better to give too much than too little.

No department of the Indian administration comes into closer touch with the people and more directly affects, for good or evil, the prosperity of the country, the contentment of the agricultural classes, and the stability of British rule, than that which is connected with the periodical assessment of the land-tax. The Officers to whom the duty is entrusted are invariably picked men, the cream of the services, though perhaps not always sufficiently ripened and chastened by experience. When the principles for their guidance were first laid down, the Government declared its wish and intention to be that the efforts of the Revenue-Officers should be chiefly directed, not to any general and extensive enhancement of the assessment, but to the objects of equalising the public burdens and of ascertaining and recording the rights of all persons and classes claiming an interest in the land or its produce. Once well and thoroughly done, this record does not need frequent revision. The questions with which it deals belong rather to the courts of law. So it has come about that the increase of assessment has risen from the subordinate to the prime place in settlement work. Indeed it is now an accepted principle that no revision is made unless a large increase of revenue is expected to result.

As a rule the assessments are fair and moderate. Such too has been the prosperity of the country, that while the revenue from the land has enormously increased, its incidence on the area of cultivation is less than it was more than half a century ago, when the principles of assessment were first laid down. But it does not follow that the tax is more easily paid than before. There are many more mouths to feed for one thing. With facilities of communication and increase of purchaseable commodities the standard of living among the peasantry has rapidly risen. Expenses of cultivation have largely increased. The rates of tax on the best soils also have been enhanced, while the extension of cultivation has naturally been for the most part in land of poorer quality. It is quite possible, therefore, that a cultivator may now find more difficulty in paying a low rate upon a large estate than he did in paying a higher rate on his most profitable land.

In these days, when money is sorely needed to meet on every hand the growing demand for improvements, not to speak of the military sieve into which so much of it is poured, there is a strong temptation to force up the assessments. It is a dangerous policy. The mischief of over-assessment is insidious. The millions of India are as yet voiceless. It is not the cry of the tillers of the soil that is borne on the Press. They suffer in silence, and their sorrows reach the ear of authority only when the mischief is done—when the wells get out of gear, when the cultivation grows slovenly, when the transfers of land to the moneyed classes are so frequent as to attract official notice, when men begin to leave their ancestral homes, when perhaps the seeds of revolution have been sown. Great as the development of India has been, it is much retarded by the want of agricultural capital. In spite of all her material improvements—new industries, unexampled growth of trade, and great addition to the general wealth—India is almost a purely agricultural country. But she is no longer the sole consumer of her own produce. She is coming every day into wider competition with other agricultural countries in the markets of the world. If she is to succeed, old methods must give way to better, and capital must be accumulated to provide the improvements. For this a margin of profit must always be left to the landowner. A system of assessment which periodically dips into every increase requires to be carefully supervised at all times. One injudicious turn of the screw may do mischief to a District which cannot be repaired in one or two generations.

Life among the rural population gave John Lawrence a strong affection for the sturdy yeoman, a sympathy with him in his difficulties, and a respect for his honest, manly independence, which he never lost. Half his time was spent in tents among the people, not in office 'from ten to four by the regulation clock.' Every corner of his charge was visited. He was accessible all day and at any hour to every one who wished to see him. Soon after he joined at Delhi the system of administration was considerably changed. Hitherto everything had been managed politically by the Resident and Chief Commissioner of Delhi, in whom vested the superintendence of the revenue, the police, and civil and criminal justice, under such orders as the Governor-General might from time to time prescribe. In 1832 the office of Resident was abolished, and the control was vested in the Supreme Courts of Justice and the Board of Revenue in the North-Western Provinces. The ordinary laws and regulations were not formally introduced, but the Commissioner and the Officers acting under him were required to 'ordinarily conform to the principles and spirit of the Regulations,' and to act according to justice, equity, and good conscience in cases for which no specific rules existed.

This was the foundation of what was afterwards developed in the Punjab into the 'Non-Regulation system.' It introduced into the Delhi Territory more law and order than had heretofore prevailed, and practically gave Lawrence the opportunity he wanted to fix his own impress on a new state of things. Associating with the people in daily intimacy, listening to their petitions, ministering to their sick, sometimes nursing them with his own hands, always ready to listen to anybody, seeing everything with his own eyes, his character was formed and he laid the foundation of the eminence to which he afterwards rose. He belonged to a class of District Officer for whom there is no longer any room in our more elaborate and highly-organised system of government in India. The species is as extinct as the mastodon or the megalosaurus.

After eight years of this life in the Delhi Territory, John Lawrence was appointed to be Settlement Officer in Etáwah. He never cared for the place, which he described as a 'hole' in which he was nearly buried. The work too was tame after what he had been accustomed to. He joined the appointment in November 1838, and before twelve months were over he was prostrated by fever, which nearly proved fatal, and compelled him to return to England, where he arrived in June 1840. So ended his first period of Indian service.

CHAPTER III

Commissioner and Chief Commissioner.

This little book is not intended to be a personal biography of John Lawrence. An able pen has written that at length. What I am endeavouring to picture is the Indian environment in which he lived and acted, his relation to the principal events of his time, and his position in the development of the constitutional principles on which the government of India is now conducted. These are of course entwined with the personal events of his life. But it will be convenient, both here and in subsequent chapters, to dismiss purely biographical matters in a very brief summary.

John Lawrence spent two years and three months in England and on the Continent in search of health (1840–42). His fever, of which he had a dangerous relapse in Calcutta on his way home, returned with such severity at Naples, towards the end of his leave, that the doctors advised him not to go back to India. But go he must, if it were only to die. And he did not go alone. On 26th August, 1841, he was married to Harriet Catherine Hamilton, daughter of the Rev

Richard Hamilton, Rector of Culdaff, in county Donegal—'the most important and certainly the happiest step in my life,' he says. Sailing from Southampton on 1st October, 1842, they arrived in Bombay by the overland route on 14th November. After a slow and difficult journey to Upper India by way of Nágpur and Allahábád, John Lawrence found himself appointed to the old familiar scenes of Delhi. The Kábul War was just over, and he had the joy of embracing his brother George, recently rescued from captivity. At Delhi he remained, first as Civil and Sessions Judge, and then as Magistrate and Collector, till the spring of 1846, when he was summoned by Lord Hardinge to be Commissioner of the country acquired from the Sikhs in the Jálandhar Doáb, and was thus translated to the thick of the stirring events which led to the annexation of the Punjab to the British dominions.

It is not my intention to narrate these events, even in brief. They are a thrice-told tale. Lord Hardinge, when on his way to the frontier, in daily expectation of the outbreak of war with the Sikhs, had met John Lawrence at Delhi in November 1845. Hardinge's discerning and soldierly eye had taken the measure of the young Magistrate, the 'vehement, swift-riding man,' with the honest and eager face, careless of dress and appearances—who seemed never to count any work too hard, or to think any duty too little to be done with his own hand—who knew every man in the place and every inch of his District, its condition, its capabilities, its resources, and its requirements. He noted him then and there as the man for his purpose should occasion arise. Nor did Lawrence fail him.

Taken aback by the determined resistance of the Khálsa[1] troops in the first battles on the banks of the Sutlej, crippled by the loss of a seventh of our army. paralysed by the exhaustion of the artillery ammunition, the want of heavy guns, and the deficiency of supplies, which the Cis-Sutlej[2] feudatories began to withhold, the English were reduced to inactivity for a time after the desperate battle of Firozsháh, and were unable to follow up their victories. A note of personal appeal from the Governor-General enlisted the energies and local knowledge of Lawrence in the provision of transport for the military stores from the Delhi magazine. A train of four thousand carts, each driven by its owner, was speedily organised. It made its journey of over two hundred miles to the front, and arrived, 'without any straggling or deserting, without the failure of a man, a wheel, or a bullock, in time for the battle of Sobráon[3].' On 9th February, 1845, the train filed into camp. On the 10th was won the crowning victory, which broke and scattered the Khálsa army and resulted in the establishment of a

[1] This name is derived from the Arabic *Khálisa*. It signifies *one's own, pure property*; thence, *the Guru's* (*or God's*) *own, special property*. See Trumpp's *Adi-Granth*, p. xci, note. As we should say, God's chosen or peculiar people.

[2] From the point of view of the Government at Calcutta, the country on the left bank of the river has acquired the name of Cis-Sutlej; that on the right, Trans-Sutlej.

[3] Sir R. Temple's *Lord Lawrence*, p. 25.

British Protectorate at Lahore and the incorporation in the British dominions of all the country, hill and plain, situated between the Beas and the Sutlej.

To the administration of this country Lawrence was now summoned. 'Send me up John Lawrence!' was Hardinge's reply to the Lieutenant-Governor of the North-Western Provinces, who wished to have a man of his own selection. The beginning of March 1846 saw him at his post. Here, with intervals during which he acted as Resident at Lahore for his brother Henry, or took his work in addition to his own, he laboured with his wonted method, resolute self-sacrifice, vigilant activity, love of the people, and single-minded devotion to duty, till the Khálsa once more struck a blow for independence and was beaten, and the kingdom of Ranjít Singh became the frontier province of our Indian Empire.

The Trans-Sutlej Territory, which John Lawrence was thus suddenly called upon to govern, is a land of singular beauty and fertility. From the banks of the Beas and Sutlej, an unbroken plain extends with a gentle ascent to the foot of the Himálăyas, whence the country rises in a receding series of mountains and valleys, higher and ever higher, to the great snow peaks which separate India from Tibet. Three of the great rivers of the Punjab—the Beas, the Rávi, and the Chenáb—take their rise in these mountain-ranges. The products are as varied as the aspect of the country. The valleys are abundantly watered by mountain streams. Kángra rice is the finest in Upper

India, while Kángra tea [1]—a product introduced since the British occupation—finds growing favour alike in the markets of Central Asia and in Mincing Lane.

The population varies in language, religion, and type. In the plains are the Játs and other agricultural tribes of the ordinary Hindu family. On the extreme North, in the valleys of Láhul and Spiti, the Mongolian element predominates over the Indian, the language is Tibetan, and the religion is Buddhism largely adulterated with Hindu ideas and demonology and spirit-worship. In the lower intervening ranges are the Rájputs of Kángra, descendants of the Sun and Moon, with genealogies that lose themselves in the mists of pre-historic times, but which are said to be authentically traced for more than two thousand years.

In the seventh century of our era, when Hiuen Tsiang, the Chinese pilgrim, passed through India, a prince of the Katoch family was ruling the kingdom of Jálandhara (Che-lan-t'o-lo). Hiuen Tsiang, who made a halt of four months, describes [2] the people as brave and impetuous, and the land as favourable for the cultivation of cereals and producing much rice, with thick and umbrageous forests and abundance of fruits and flowers. At the present day there are in the Jálandhar territory the representatives of eleven principalities, the debris of once powerful dynasties. Three of them—Mandi, Chamba, and Suket—are still

[1] In the years 1890 and 1891 the area under tea-cultivation in the Punjab was 9,229 acres, of which 9,177 are in the Kángra District, the other fifty-two acres being in Simla.

[2] Beal's *Buddhist Records of the Western World*, vol. i. p. 175.

Ruling Houses; the others are only titled nobility. It is the cadets who have survived as Ruling Chiefs. Naturally their portions were in the more inaccessible hills and less fertile valleys. And to this they owe it that, though they lost bits of territory and had to pay tribute to the Sikhs, they escaped the political extinction which overtook the elder branches in the more open districts when, in an evil hour, Ranjít Singh was called in to help to repel a Gúrkha invasion. Having once gained a footing in these principalities, the 'Lion of the Punjab,' bit by bit, by fraud and violence, reduced to subjection all the lower hills between the Rávi and the Sutlej.

When the country was annexed to the British dominions the old Chieftains expected great things. But the policy of the day was to maintain the status as we found it and to restore nothing which the Sikhs had taken. Chiefs whom we found to be still ruling were maintained in their States subject to tribute, but those who had lost their sovereign powers did not get them back. Nothing else was to have been expected from the known antecedents and training of Lawrence. To him the idea of these Chiefs being royal families and crowned heads was ridiculous; they were only petty barons. 'I certainly think it would be madness in us,' he wrote, 'to give them back much of their old power and extensive possessions. Continue to them the jágírs held under the Sikhs, and if they have done good service in the war, make them a money present, or even give them an annual stipend in cash, but do not give them more power. . . . It is a mistake to think that by making Rájás and Chiefs powerful you attach the country. One lakh given in the reduction of assessments and making people comfortable and happy in their homes is better than three lakhs given to Rájás.'

The Rájás were bitterly disappointed. Only in name could the position assigned to them be the same as under the Sikhs. A British Jágírdar is a mere receiver of rents or revenue. A Sikh Jágírdar was still a petty Prince in his estates, with immense power and prestige. So long as his tribute was paid or his service rendered to his government, he might do very much as he liked. He could still dispense a rude justice or injustice; he could levy benevolences; he could take cesses on property, on trade, and even on domestic occurrences; he was served by unpaid labour. All this was swept clean away by the annexation. It followed naturally that the Chiefs were discontented as well as disappointed. The barons sulked in their ancestral halls and bided their time. When the Sikh nation rose and made their last struggle for independence, the emissaries of the Khálsa incited the disestablished Princes to join them, and promised the restoration of their little Kingdoms if the British power should be overthrown. John Lawrence was prepared for this. 'After Hazára,' he wrote[1], 'the elements of discord prevail to a greater extent in Kángra than in any other District of the

[1] *Life of Reynell Taylor*, p. 220.

Punjab.' The country bristled with forts. Every little palace was a fortified building. Kángra and Núrpur had a fabled reputation. In the proverbs of the people, he who ruled Kángra ruled the hills. Years afterwards, in the height of the Mutiny, Lawrence wrote that if by any misadventure Kángra should be lost to us, a general insurrection of the hill people would almost certainly follow.

In 1848 the Rájás of Kángra, Jaswán, and Datárpur, with the Wazír of Núrpur and other discontented leaders, backed by the prestige and influence of Bedi Bikrama Singh, the descendant of Guru Nának, and the chief-priest of the Sikh religion, raised the standard of rebellion and proclaimed that the English rule had ceased. But they had cast in their lot with a losing cause. With a small force and some raw levies, and within a very few hours, Lawrence and his Officers were upon them wherever rebellion showed its head.

'By the orders of John Lawrence,' writes Robert Cust, who, as one of his subordinates, had charge of the District of Hoshiárpur, 'I issued a Proclamation[1] to

[1] This Proclamation, so vigorous and characteristic both of Lawrence and his men, is worth preserving :—

'Robert Cust, the Deputy-Commissioner and Superintendent of the District of Hoshiárpur, to all the principal landowners in the district, sent by special messenger to each separately.

'*Camp, Hájípur, Nov.* 28, 1848.

'I expect, and am fully confident, that you are in your own villages, and have kept clear of any rebellion. If any of your relations have joined the rebels, write to them to come back before blood is shed : if they do so, their fault will be forgiven. Consider that I have in person visited every one of your villages, and I know the position of every one of you : what is your injury I consider

the headmen of the villages to meet us at different points of our hasty march to grapple with the insurgents. At each halting-place they were assembled in scores, and when a sword and a pen were placed before them to select the instrument by which they wished to be ruled, the pen was grasped with enthusiasm. With the genius of a general, Lawrence planned and carried into execution this bloodless campaign, where delays would have been fatal.' In a few days all was over; the rebel leaders were made prisoners and sent into exile, their palaces and fortresses were razed to the ground, and the estates which had been continued to them were confiscated.

'This campaign,' Edwin Arnold justly observes, 'has attracted too little regard from the annalists of the period: as a horseman who plays no fine tricks of

mine: what is gain to you I consider my gain. The rule of the British is in favour of the agriculturist. If your lands are heavily assessed, tell me so, and I will relieve you: if you have any grievance, let me know it, and I will try to remove it: if you have any plans, let me know them, and I will give you my advice: *if you will excite rebellion, as I live, I will severely punish you.* I have ruled this district three years by the sole agency of the pen, and if necessary I will rule it by the sword. God forbid that matters should come to that. This trouble affects your families and your prosperity. The Rájás of the country get up the disturbance, but it is the landowners whose lands are plundered. Consider what I have said, and talk it over with your relations, and bring all back from rebellion, and when my camp comes in your neighbourhood, attend at once in person, and tell those who have joined the rebellion to return to me, as children who have committed a fault return to their fathers, and their faults will be forgiven them. Let this be known in the valley of Jaswán, and be of good cheer. In two days I shall be in the midst of you with a force which you will be unable to resist.'

horsemanship, nor trifles with the hot temper of his steed, wins less applause from an idle eye than the showy rider, who provokes the fury which he has then to check.' The position of the rebels on the right flank of our main army which was operating against the Sikhs made their immediate suppression imperative. Had John Lawrence not acted promptly and on his own responsibility, the rebellion would have assumed a formidable aspect. Viewed by itself, however, the offence of rising, under overwhelming temptation, against a foreign rule which had been established for little more than two years, was not an unpardonable one. In the lapse of time it has been forgiven. The survivors of the families have been permitted to return, and some of them have been reinstated in a portion of their old family domains. When Her Majesty the Queen was proclaimed Empress of India, the Jaswán estate was restored, as an act of grace, to the great-grandson of the Rájá who rebelled. And some years later, before I left the Punjab, I was instrumental in obtaining permission for the grandson, who was only a lad of twenty when he went 'out,' to return to his old home.

John Lawrence found his views justified. The people were contented and did not rise. What had been a sore grievance to the Rájás was a blessing to them. The hand of the Sikh was very heavy on the property and lives of men. George Forster[1], writing

[1] *Journey from Bengal to England through the northern part of India*, &c. London, 1798.

of this very part of the country about fifty years before, thanks God that, 'unhurt by Sicques, tygers or thieves, he is safely lodged in Nourpour.' For some years before our rule the people had been severely ground down by the local governor, Sheikh Imám-ud-dín. But now the lion and the lamb could drink at the same fountain. The lamb had no fear; the people were contented. In March 1846 the country had been annexed; before the harvest was ripe the greater part of it was summarily assessed to land-revenue. A large reduction was made on the revenue levied by the Sikhs, and the demand was fixed for three years. Unauthorised cesses, benevolences, and perquisites were swept away. A light money assessment was substituted for payments in grain. These measures were eminently successful, although the summary settlement was found in some villages to have been pitched too high and remissions had to be granted. It was in the Jálandhar District that Lawrence gave George Christian the instructions to assess low, which I have already quoted. In the Kángra District, George Barnes, who made the regular settlement three years afterwards, estimated that the summary settlement had 'added from fifteen to twenty per cent. to each man's income.'

In the virgin soil of the Trans-Sutlej States, John Lawrence, with his Assistants, Cust and Scott and Barnes and Lake, was able to sow good seed broadcast. It was a new country; he had a free hand, and could mould the administration very much as he pleased. 'I want to put my stamp on it,' he wrote, 'that in after-times people may look back and recall my Ráj with satisfaction. No portion of our Empire promises better than it does.' The system of civil administration introduced was of the simplest kind. A few Rules of Procedure were drawn up for the guidance of the Civil Officers. The law administered was the *lex loci*, when not repugnant to principles of natural justice or to equity or good policy. In cases not specially provided for, the Regulations in force in the Company's territories were to prevail, as far as circumstances would admit, and in doubtful cases instructions were to be asked for. Religious liberty was proclaimed. Mussulmán, Hindu, Sikh, and Christian were alike protected. All were free to observe their own religious and social customs, but none were permitted to injure or meddle with their neighbours in the observance of theirs. Once more the call to public prayer, which the Sikhs had silenced, awoke the dawn from the minarets of the mosque. But in vain was the veil of religious sanction thrown over crimes like *satí* and child-murder. These were put down with a strong and stern hand.

The Bedis [1], the priestly class among the Sikhs,

[1] The Bedis are descendants of Lakshmi Dás, the second son of Guru Nának, the founder of the Sikh religion. In the *Granth* (Book, Bible) the killing of daughters is strictly forbidden. 'A true Sikh may have no intercourse with those who kill their daughters.' —Trumpp's *Adi-Granth*, pp. cxv and cxvi. Also Cunningham's *Sikhs*, p. 363: 'With the slayers of daughters whoever has intercourse, him do I curse.' 'Whoever takes food from the slayers of daughters shall die unabsolved.'

were most addicted to the crime of female infanticide, notwithstanding the fact that it is sternly forbidden in their sacred books. But it was prevalent also among Rájputs and other Hindu castes, and even among some classes of Muhammadans. But, whatever the predisposing cause—whether it was religious, whether it was founded on peculiar tenets and considerations of caste, whether it was avarice, or whether it was pride of birth—whatever it was, the crime had to be stamped out. Proclamations were issued that it would be treated and punished as murder; the chief men of tribes were called on to suppress it; an annual census of the inhabitants, male and female, of all villages and tribes known to be addicted to it, was prescribed; and honorary rewards were promised to those who should distinguish themselves in the crusade against the inhuman practice.

The years spent in the Jálandhar Doáb were the happiest in Lawrence's official life. His domestic circle was not broken up by the separations incident to Indian service. His work was thoroughly congenial to him, and he was his own master. Boehm has chosen the sword and pen incident of this period as the subject for a statue[1]. The artist represents John Lawrence as offering to the people the choice between enforced submission and willing obedience:

[1] This statue was presented by Sir Edgar Boehm to the Municipality of Lahore, and has been erected on a commanding site. It was unveiled by the present writer in the Jubilee year of Her Majesty's reign, on 30th March, 1887.

'By which will ye be governed—the pen or the sword?' The pen prevailed; but none the less was the sword ever in reserve, though sheathed. In their first Punjab Report the Board of Administration were able to say that the Trans-Sutlej States were the most prosperous, the most easily managed, and the most profitable of the territories under their control.

From these scenes of peaceful and philanthropic labour Lawrence was called away to take part in the administration of the territories which the Second Punjab War laid at our feet. The events are matters of general history. Lord Dalhousie succeeded Lord Hardinge on 12th January, 1848. The Empire was in profound peace. But the new Governor-General had only been four months in power when Vans Agnew and Anderson, deserted by their Sikh escort, were murdered at Múltán and the Khálsa army began once more to raise its head. Herbert Edwardes, with no resources but his courage, his soldiership, and a few raw levies, defeated the local governor Múlráj and cooped him up in the fort of Múltán. But the summer heat was on, and the English forces could not move. In an Indian crisis delay is fatal. Disaffection gains head, the wavering fall away, and friends hesitate to declare themselves. Before the British troops were able to take the field in the autumn, the whole Sikh nation was up in arms and had combined with their hereditary enemies, the Afgháns, in an alliance for our destruction. The Punjab had to be reconquered: the Sikh army passed under the yoke, and all that remained of the Sikh Kingdom from the previous war passed under the sceptre of the Queen of England (1849).

For the administration of this new country, together with the territory previously acquired on both sides of the Sutlej, Dalhousie appointed a Board of Three—the president, Sir Henry Lawrence, and two members, John Lawrence and Charles Mansel, the latter of whom was succeeded by Robert Montgomery. It was on this Board that Sir Charles Napier penned his savage epigram—'Boards indeed rarely have any talent, and that of the Punjab offers no exception to the rule.' But the world has pronounced another verdict on the labours of these eminent men. From the first, the Board was intended to be a temporary arrangement, whereby Lord Dalhousie could combine the heart and rare gifts of Henry Lawrence with the clear head and strong hand of John in reducing the new province to order. It is not my part to draw any comparison between the two heroic brothers—'both illustrious,' as Edwin Arnold says, 'in a House which, like the Fabian, has a prescription to serve and save the State.' Their story is well known. John admitted his brother to be a keener and higher intellect than himself and to have a greater 'grip' on men. Henry admitted that, in a school of able men such as are seldom to be seen anywhere, his chief help was in his brother John, without whom he would have had difficulty in carrying on. But they were trained in different schools and their policies were irreconcilable. When, therefore, the work of pacification was done, and the work of organisation had to begin, it is not surprising that Lord Dalhousie selected John, whose general views were in accordance with his own. Henry, the friend of every one who was 'down,' the loved, the generous, who 'got a little more for every one,' who 'fought every losing battle for the old Chiefs and Jághírdars, with entire disregard to his own interest [1],' left the Punjab, amid an outburst of universal lamentation, to write his name imperishably on another page of Indian history. Henceforward John Lawrence ruled supreme in the Punjab as Chief Commissioner, doing his duty with the same simplicity as of old, the same devotion and singleness of purpose, all unconscious of the fiery ordeal by which his work was soon to be tried.

[1] Raikes, *Notes on the Revolt in the North-Western Provinces of India*, p. 33.

CHAPTER IV

A Non-Regulation Province

The First Sikh War added a little over 15,000 square miles of territory to the British dominions. The Second Sikh War added a Kingdom nearly five times as large; it advanced the boundaries of our Empire to the mountain-ranges, where they remained for more than thirty years, till we crossed the Passes in search of a 'scientific frontier'; and it profoundly altered our relations to the politics of Kábul, Central Asia, and Russia.

The country is classic ground, the furthest theatre of the conquests of Alexander the Great. Almost on the same field where, nearly twenty-two centuries ago, he defeated Porus, we fought the indecisive battle of Chilianwála. Lahore, its capital, is the Labokla of Ptolemy, on the Rávi (Irávati, 'abounding in water,' Hydraotes), near where Alexander crossed. Next perhaps to Delhi, its history is interwoven with the rise and fall of dynasties in Upper India. It was the capital of a Muhammadan Kingdom long before the Mughal Empire was established. 'Lahore of great Mogul' is among the 'earth's kingdoms and their glory' disclosed to Adam by Michael the Archangel from the hill of Paradise. The reign of Akbar[1] was the time of its greatest splendour. It was famous for the curious stuffs and silk brocades issued from the imperial manufactories. There were more than a thousand workshops for shawl-weaving. Sea-going ships were made here and transported to the coast. In Akbar's time it was also a place of great literary activity. At Lahore the Emperor collected at his court poets, divines, and historians. Here were held some of those famous discussions from which Akbar sought to sublimate an eclectic religion, or perhaps only to cover his lapse from Muhammadan orthodoxy. The ruins of crumbling mosques and tombs and ancient gateways scattered for miles round the present city witness to its former extent and magnificence. Remarkable now for its well-paved and well-drained streets, Lahore, in the Sikh days, was notorious as the 'filthiest capital in India.' It is still one of the most striking Oriental cities in India, more interesting, perhaps, than even Pesháwar.

Our quarrel was with the Sikhs, not with the people of the Punjab. Although the Punjab is the home of the Sikh nation, only a fraction of the population—less than one-twelfth—is Sikh. Judged by population, the Punjab is a Muhammadan province. More than half the population is Muhammadan. But it must be borne in mind that the Sikh is a Hindu,

[1] See Gladwin's *Ayeen Akbery*, vol. i. pp. 13, 63, 105, and 250, and vol. ii. p. 119.

and his religion is only a phase of Hinduism. The Játs furnish most of the converts, and it is no uncommon thing to find in the same family one brother a Hindu and another a Sikh. The Muhammadans too partake largely of Hindu blood, their ancestors having been converted to Islám, forcibly or otherwise. The true home of the Sikh is the Mánjha, or 'middle-land,' the central portion of the plain between the Beas and the Rávi, of which the capital is Amritsar. This small tract of country contains a third of the Sikh population, the rest, known as the Málwá Sikhs, being distributed for the most part over the Districts south of the Sutlej.

It was with the Sikh army and the Sikhs that we came into collision in 1848. The movement was a solid and national one on their part. From the Mánjha the people flocked in thousands to the standard raised by Sardár Chhatar Singh. Many of the leaders were nobles who had signed a treaty with us only eighteen months before. The Commander-in-Chief of the rebel army had been a member of the Council of Regency. But over most of the Punjab the Government which we were to destroy was a military despotism, established by the sword and maintained by the sword, hardly softened by the short British Protectorate. In Ranjít Singh's lifetime, the masterfulness of his genius, the prestige of conquest, the sentiment of young national life, edged off the roughness of the government. But with Ranjít Singh the false glory departed. Indeed it is a marvel how the country could have endured so long the burden of taxation we removed. In addition to the land-tax, the Sikh government imposed duties upon no fewer than forty-eight classes of articles of trade and commerce—many, indeed most of them, the produce of domestic industry. For these we substituted four new taxes—on salt, on drugs and spirits, stamps, and ferry-tolls—which brought in the same revenue, while they freed the produce of the soil, which had already paid land-tax, cut away a network of customs lines which throttled the commerce of the country, and delivered the people from unlimited extortion. 'Our true policy,' John Lawrence wrote, 'is to give up every restriction that we can possibly do without and retain the land-tax. By this means we conciliate the masses, and especially the industrial classes. Customs levies are harassing in all countries; in this country they are intolerable' (1849).

Once more John Lawrence had virgin soil to cultivate. 'I should like to fix my own impress on the administration,' he wrote; 'I desire earnestly to shew what a man bred and educated as a civilian can do in a new country.' He had a fine staff of Officers—picked men like Montgomery, Macleod, Edward Thornton, Cust, Barnes, and others—the flower of the civil service of the North-Western Provinces. And there was the splendid school trained by his brother Henry. These men made the Punjab administration famous. All of them were young. Edwardes was little more than thirty, with the laurels of Múltán fresh upon him.

John Lawrence himself was only forty-two when he was made Chief Commissioner. Lord Dalhousie, who inspired and controlled them, the youngest Governor-General ever appointed to India, was only 37 in 1849. Many of them too were brave and tried soldiers, bearing the honourable scars of battle. Edwardes carried a bullet-wound, and Reynell Taylor three sabre-cuts, from the field of Múdki. Nicholson, when a mere stripling, had distinguished himself by prodigies of valour at Ghazní before he obeyed the orders to surrender and yield himself to what seemed at the time a hopeless captivity. He had been through Chilianwála and Gujrát and in Gilbert's pursuit, and was only thirty-four when he met the soldier's death in the assault of Delhi.

Fearing no responsibility and shirking no labour, there was perhaps a tendency in the young men to act too much on their own initiative, or, as Lord Dalhousie put it, 'to consider themselves as Governor-General at least.' Edwardes had already drawn Dalhousie's fire upon himself:—'I will not stand it in quieter times for half an hour, and will come down unmistakably upon any one of them who may "try it on," from Major Edwardes, C.B., down to the latest-enlisted General-Ensign-Plenipotentiary on the establishment.' Perhaps the kingly vision of Dalhousie was a little distorted by his imperiousness. But this fertility of initiative, this disregard of formalities, this readiness to accept responsibility without usurping it, stood us well in the after-days of trial.

It was the fashion at one time to sneer at the Punjab school and their rough-and-ready methods, as if what was done quickly and done with least technicality of form must necessarily be badly done. No use, it was said, to gallop out twenty miles to decide a case if you give a wrong decision at the end. As if it were any better to give a wrong decision in court from an arm-chair! But in fact the cases were simple and dependent on local custom, and they were investigated in the face of crowds who knew the facts and under conditions far more favourable to the discovery of truth than the oaths of the court and the cross-examination of the barrister. The accessibility of the Officers and the personal influence they gained did more for the pacification of the country than regiments of soldiers. In time the Non-Regulation system came to be synonymous with all that is best for the government of a newly-conquered country. After the Mutiny of 1857, when the whole fabric of administration in Upper India had to be reconstructed, Lord Canning drew some of his best men from the Punjab, and when remonstrated with, only answered that he must take more.

The Non-Regulation system means, as I have already explained, that the administration should be conducted according to the principles and spirit of the Regulations, but not fettered by the letter, and that justice, equity, and good conscience should speak when the law is silent. The principle underlying it is the kernel of despotism. It assumes that in conquered countries the Executive Government is independent of the Legislature, and can make laws and rules for itself as the Queen does in a crown colony. This assumption continued to be acted upon till the passing of the India Councils Act in 1861, since which time it has been held that the Government possesses no other legislative powers in Non-Regulation provinces than in other parts of the country. From this point of view, the distinction between Regulation provinces and Non-Regulation provinces has become a matter of history.

Dalhousie proclaimed that over those who should live as obedient and peaceful subjects the British Government would rule with mildness and benevolence. He declared it to be his wish to uphold Native institutions and practices as far as they are consistent with the distribution of justice to all classes. He did not desire to introduce our voluminous laws into this new province. But he was persuaded there were few parts of the country which would not be benefited by the gradual introduction of the British system of administration at the earliest possible period. Three principles characterised the Non-Regulation system adopted by John Lawrence. *First*, the country was mapped out into Districts, so small in respect of area, population, and revenue, that it was possible for the Civil Officers to gain a complete knowledge of them and to become personally acquainted with all the men of mark and influence. *Secondly*, every civil functionary, from the highest to the lowest, in due order of subordination, was vested with judicial, fiscal, and magisterial powers, so as to secure concentration of authority and undivided responsibility. *Thirdly*, the laws and procedure introduced were of the simplest kind, and were based as far as might be on Native customs and institutions.

John Lawrence impressed his own individuality on all his Officers—his vigour, promptitude, and determination to do the work before him with singleness of purpose. Responsibility was undivided, and the delegation of power went down in an unbroken chain of subordination, so that the influence of the central authority was directly felt by every Officer and to the extremities of the province. The Chief Commissioner knew his men. For honest mistakes there was toleration; for idleness or the incompetence of ignorance there was none. Every man was required to know his work and to do it, and to see that the men under him knew and did it too.

It was to John Lawrence, Edwardes has told us, that we owe the key-stone of the Non-Regulation arch —the union of judicial, revenue, and magisterial powers in all Officers in their various degrees. He had a great objection to the civil and revenue work being separated, and considered it ruinous to the tenures of the country. The arrangement he made was admirably adapted to the actual needs of the Punjab at that time. Under the Sikh rule the people had never been accustomed to separation of functions. All powers centred in the Kárdár. For us to have introduced a multiplicity of authorities would only have perplexed them. As matters were arranged, they knew exactly to whom to carry their complaints, and from whom to receive orders. The means of redressing their wrongs was brought to their door.

The system gave the Civil Officers a hold on their Districts they could not otherwise have got. The District Officer, or Deputy-Commissioner as he was called, and his Assistants were expected to be everywhere, to know everything affecting the welfare of their charge, to be accessible to the people at all times and in all places, and to be able to check the reports of Native officials by personal knowledge. I served my apprenticeship as a Civil Officer in the Punjab in those days. Looking back at them after an interval of five-and-thirty years, I seem still to have a sort of feeling of ubiquity. A good stable was an essential equipment. If in the remotest corner of the District there occurred a cow-riot or an affray or a murder or a big burglary, the Deputy-Commissioner or an Assistant had to be on the spot. If cholera broke out, every village affected had to be visited. No remission of revenue was ever granted without a personal inspection of the land and the crops. Nothing that affected the welfare of the District or the contentment of the people was too insignificant for personal attention. It was an unwritten law that the Civil Officers should see things with their own eyes, do things with their own hands, and enquire into things for themselves. Thus they came to know the people, the people learned to know them, and a grip was got on the country which the Mutiny of 1857 did not loosen.

Perhaps the most striking feature of the Punjab administration was the simplicity of its laws and its legal machinery. Under the Sikh rule there was no written law. Disputes were for the most part settled by arbitrators in accordance with tribal custom or the usage of trade. 'The unwritten penal code contained but two penalties—fine and mutilation. There was scarcely any crime, from larceny up to murder, for which impunity might not be purchased by the payment of a fine[1].' Cattle-lifters were liable to be hamstrung, robbers had their hands cut off, and offences like adultery and seduction were punished by slitting the nose. When I began my service in the Punjab there were many of these mutilated wretches wandering about and subsisting on the gifts of the charitable.

The patriarchal administration of John Lawrence has sometimes been spoken of as government without law. But this was not the case. He held that rules and regulations were as necessary for the good management of a newly-conquered country as in our older provinces. No doubt everything depended on a vigorous executive, and some of the best executive Officers were more conspicuous for zeal and energy and devotion to duty than for legal knowledge and training. But it was no fault of his if there was uncertainty as to the law. The Chief Commissioner required the executive to be guided by law and rule,

[1] *First Punjab Administration Report*, par. 29.

when law and rule could be ascertained. Even in the time of the Mutiny, when, if ever, there might have been excuse for neglect, the Chief Commissioner was never tolerant of arbitrary conduct, though many high-handed things had of necessity to be done for the preservation of the State. 'So far, indeed,' says Sir James Stephen [1], 'was it from being true that the great authority of Lord Lawrence could be quoted in favour of personal government as against government by law, that it would be much more like the truth to say that Lord Lawrence's administration of the Punjab afforded the clearest proof that could be given, not only of the necessity of having laws to govern by, but of the superiority of simple and scientific laws over cumbrous ones.' After annexation, the administration was guided in civil matters by the simple Rules which had been adopted in the Sutlej Territories, and in criminal matters by the principles of the Regulations as stated in the ordinary text-books, a large discretion being left to Magistrates to frame their proceedings so as to suit the circumstances of the country. The people were unused to technicalities and legal refinements, and could not have understood them. Great importance was attached to local and social customs so far as they did not conflict with morality or public policy. The Punjab contains a great diversity of tribes and races, with corresponding diversity of customs, which are not covered by the Hindu and Muhammadan law of the text-books. In

[1] Speech in Legislative Council, 27th June, 1871.

the province generally, and especially among the Muhammadan tribes of the frontier, these customs have often a sanction more powerful than law, and the breach of them can be atoned for only by blood.

John Lawrence recognised at once the impossibility of dealing with divers races by a uniform law imported by a foreign government, and the difficulty of deciding 'as to what rule will be observed, what rights upheld, what laws introduced, under what conditions and to what extent each law will be superseded by custom[1].' He therefore caused a compendious abstract of legal principles to be prepared with special reference to the known peculiarities of the country and people. This abstract was practically accepted as the Civil Code of the Punjab, and so suitable was it found to the circumstances of a new country, that it was afterwards introduced by the Government of India into Oudh and other Non-Regulation provinces as the basis of the judicial administration. To Sir Robert Montgomery and Sir Richard Temple belongs the honour of compiling this remarkable work. It 'does not pretend even to an attempt at the codification of Civil Law,' but it is an admirable Code nevertheless. While it recognises local and tribal usages, its general principles are drawn from the Regulations, the Hindu and Muhammadan law, English law, and various other sources. Even the

[1] Abstract Principles of Law circulated for the guidance of Officers employed in the administration of Civil Justice in the Punjab. Preface, p. vi.

Code Napoleon is made to do service. It provided that custom is to prevail over the ordinary Hindu and Muhammadan law in the decision of such matters as inheritance, property of women, marriage, divorce, adoption, and the like, which intimately affect the dearest interests of the people. At the same time it introduced some enlightened provisions, which anticipated by years the course of general legislation. Among these may be mentioned the recognition of the re-marriage of Hindu widows, limited liability in partnership, and the abolition of usury laws. Its Rules of Procedure were simple, free from technicalities, and so framed that, by bringing the parties face to face, by ensuring that they understood their own interests, by endeavouring to effect compromises and so on, all means of amicable settlement were exhausted before the parties became involved in the toils of litigation.

This simple Code has long been superseded by the progress of the country. But it was admirably suited to the time when it was framed. It prevented the province from being bound in the fetters of intricate Muhammadan and Hindu law and overshadowed by the cloud of commentaries. It was a bulwark against the flood of English law which otherwise would inevitably have followed the establishment of British courts. On the one hand it saved social and tribal customs from being needlessly swept away; on the other hand it admitted of their growth and improvement. And not the least of the benefits which it conferred on the Punjab—it compelled the Legislature to provide in its future laws for local and provincial usage. It is now the established law of the Punjab that mercantile usages and local customs affecting the family life of the people and the disposition of their property shall be valid and shall be recognised by the courts of law, unless they be contrary to justice, equity, or good conscience. Among the legacies that John Lawrence left to the province he so vigorously governed, this is perhaps one of the most beneficent.

It is not my purpose to recount the measures adopted for the pacification of the Punjab, the organisation of its government, and the development of its resources. How the country was disarmed, how the frontier was defended, how violent crime was put down, how the coinage was reformed—these and many other things of interest are set forth in the First Punjab Administration Report with an ability and a literary skill that make it the most readable of Blue Books. In a review which did insufficient justice to the magnificent works of material improvement, the civil and military buildings, the bridges, the network of roads, the plantations, the wells, canals, and works of irrigation, which had been executed under the direction of Colonel Robert Napier, afterwards Lord Napier of Magdala, who was then John Lawrence's Chief Engineer, the Court of Directors[1] wrote:—

'In the short period which has elapsed since the Punjab

[1] Political Letter, 26th October (No. 42), 1853.

became a part of the British dominions, results have been achieved such as could scarcely have been hoped for as the reward of many years of well-directed exertions. The formidable army which it had required so many battles to subdue has been quietly disbanded, and the turbulent soldiery have settled to industrious pursuits. Peace and security reign throughout the country, and the amount of crime is as small as in our best administered territories. Justice has been made accessible, without costly formalities, to the whole population. Industry and commerce have been set free. A great mass of oppressive and burthensome taxation has been abolished. Money rents have been substituted for payments in kind, and a settlement of the land revenue has been completed in nearly the whole country, at a considerable reduction on the former amount. In the settlement the best lights of recent experience have been turned to the utmost account, and the various errors committed in a more imperfect state of our knowledge of India have been carefully avoided. . . . It is a source of just pride to us that our services, civil and military, should have afforded men capable, in so short a time, of carrying into full effect such a series of enlightened and beneficent measures.'

This catalogue of results in general terms must suffice. What was the secret of such success? It lay not entirely in the fact that Dalhousie's kingly hand directed and controlled the administration. Nor in the fact that the Chief Commissioner and his Officers had the experience of our older provinces to guide them. Nor yet in the fact that they were picked men, all in the prime of life or the bloom and promise of early manhood. All that was true and counted for much, but it was not everything. The secret lay rather in the spirit which moved them; and that spirit was inspired by John Lawrence and his brother. There was a unique truthfulness, simplicity, and singleness of purpose about them. Each strove to do his duty, neither courting favour nor fearing blame. They loved the people; they lived among the people and for the people. They were accessible at all times and places and were never above any kind of work. They had a respect for Native ways and institutions, and did not consider a thing bad because it was not English. They put themselves in the people's place and made the interests and the cares of the people their own, striving to identify them with the government, and create as it were a family feeling. Look at the Hoshiárpur Proclamation —'what is your injury I consider mine; what is gain to you I consider my gain; return to me, as children who have committed a fault return to their fathers, and their faults will be forgiven them.' This touch of nature did much to break down the barriers of colour and creed and national animosity. Every measure introduced was beneficent in conception and beneficent in its direct effect upon the masses of the people. This was the firm foundation on which the Punjab administration was built and which enabled it to weather the flood and the storm that were so soon and so fiercely to beat upon it. If I have not made this one thing clear, my story has been spoiled in the telling.

Eight years passed away in this beneficent work.

The province was peaceful and prosperous. Commerce grew apace with the removal of the taxes and customs barriers. Rapid extension of cultivation followed the reduction and fixity of the land-tax and the security given to life and property by the disarmament of the country. A net-work of roads, connecting the towns and villages, gave access to markets and relieved the glut and congestion that came with the first years of peace. Prices, which at first had greatly fallen, were beginning to rise, while golden harvests brought wealth to the tillers of the soil. Wages were good, and work was plentiful on the canals, roads and public buildings. The Frontier Force and the Military Police gave stirring employment to men of martial habits. Such peace and prosperity had never been known in the province within the memory of living men. All the efforts of the Government had been designed to improve the condition of the people; and they were contented. Even the Sikh laid aside his national ambitions and quietly accepted the new state of things.

The Chief Commissioner had now laboured for fourteen years as few men labour, without a day's relaxation, except a short visit to Calcutta, there to take farewell of his master and friend, Lord Dalhousie, and to be told of the well-earned honour of knighthood proposed for him. Incessant work had told on his health. Severe fever had more than once put his life in danger. He did not think he had more than three or four years of good honest work left in him, and was beginning to look to the day when he could return to England and devote himself to the interests of his family. He had been compelled in the summer months to seek a refuge from the fierce heat, at Murree in the Himálaya mountains. Here he could do more work in one day than in three at Lahore. In the Spring of 1857 he had left Lahore for this mountain retreat and had reached Ráwal Pindi, at the foot of the Hills, when his journey was arrested by the terrible news of the military revolt at Meerut, and that Delhi, the ancestral seat of the Mughals, was in the hands of the unpursued mutineers.

CHAPTER V

THE MUTINY

THERE had no doubt been warnings of the coming danger; but the issue broke on all India like a thunderbolt from a clear sky. The dangerous state of the Bengal army had long been known. The wayward genius of Sir Charles Napier had foreseen what was coming more clearly perhaps than any one else. But the rancour of his frustrated ambition lessened the weight of his warnings. Lord Ellenborough had foreshadowings of a possible mutiny. Prophetic passages might be quoted from many writers. The sagacity of Sir Henry Lawrence had enabled him even to name Delhi and Meerut as the possible theatre of catastrophe. Whether the writers expected the early realisation of their forebodings may be doubted; at all events no action was taken to anticipate such a catastrophe, although the solidarity of the great Bráhman brotherhood was being gradually broken up by the enlistment of irregular troops.

For some months before the outbreak a vague feeling prevailed that something was wrong. Mischief was in the air. Mysterious cakes passed through the villages from hand to hand. A proclamation purporting to be from the Sháh of Persia, written on a scrap of dirty paper and rudely illustrated with a naked sword and shield, announcing the approach of a Persian army to exterminate the English, was posted on the Great Mosque at Delhi. Intrigues between the King of Delhi and foreign powers were reported. The minds of the Sepoys were troubled. Family remittances began to fall off and the price of gold coins went up rapidly. Then came the story of the greased cartridges, the insubordination and mutinies at Berhampur, Barrackpur, and Lucknow, the disbandment of the regiments, the executions, the nightly fires at Lucknow, Meerut, and Ambála and other military stations, breaking out no one could discover how. There was a general feeling of insecurity. Something assuredly was coming.

But it is no reflection on the wisest to say that no one imagined that the whole army would turn as they did on their masters and strike for the restoration of a Muhammadan Empire. Lord Canning and his advisers certainly did not. The Commander in Chief certainly did not. On the 1st of May, the military authorities at Ambála were writing that there was no sign of insubordination and no reason to accuse the Sepoys of causing the nightly fires. Nor were the Punjab authorities more prescient. Neither Lawrence nor Edwardes, when negotiating the treaty with the Amír of Kábul three months before, foresaw the outbreak. When the crisis came on, nearly one-fourth of the

Punjab Frontier Force was on furlough and had to be suddenly recalled. John Lawrence himself had at one time proposed to spend the summer in Kashmír, and on the 4th of May, only one short week before the rising, he had written to Lord Canning from Siálkot a re-assuring letter as to the feeling of the Sepoys there. A universal sense of uneasiness prevailed but no one was able to interpret the signs. A royal dignity hedged the English round; the white face carried an unassailable prestige; and when the occurrences at Meerut and Delhi were first announced it would be difficult to say which feeling for a time was the stronger in the English mind—a paralysis of bewilderment at the audacity of the rising, or horror and fury at the atrocities by which it was attended.

The causes of this stupendous catastrophe have baffled investigation. Sir John Lawrence formed a decided opinion that its origin lay in the army itself, and that its proximate cause was the cartridge affair and nothing else. 'As a body,' says the Chief Commissioner [1], 'the Native army did really believe that the universal introduction of cartridges destructive to their caste was only a matter of time. They heard (and believed as they heard) that the measure had been resolved on, and that some Sepoys had been punished even by death for refusing to use the objectionable cartridges. They thought, therefore, that their only chance of escape was to band together, to

[1] Letter on the trial of the King of Delhi, Political, No. 50, dated April 29, 1858.

refuse the cartridges, and to resist if force should be attempted by the Government; and the incendiary fires at the different stations were intended by the Sepoys as a warning to their Officers and to their Government of the feelings which had taken possession of the Native army. Such truly was the origin of the mutiny.' This is the one fact that, in Sir John Lawrence's opinion, stands clearly out; the intrigues and false stories that were rife within and without the army would not have drawn the army from its allegiance, had it not been already penetrated by the unfortunate belief about the cartridges; nor would such an ill-feeling have so speedily arisen, had the army not been for years in an unsound state. There was no proof of a general conspiracy for the overthrow of the English rule; there was no evidence, even in the records of the palace at Delhi which were ransacked, that, until he was in the hands of the mutineers, the King had seriously dreamed of the restoration of his power.

But this view does not account for the phenomena. It may be admitted that, even perhaps in Oudh, the evidence is insufficient to connect the revolt with popular discontent. But in some places—at Muzaffarnagar, Sahâranpur, Farukhâbâd, and elsewhere—after the success of the military outbreak at Meerut and Delhi, the populace rose before the Sepoys. The leaders, in their Proclamations, dwelt much on alleged bad faith, earth-hunger, and interference with the Native religions, citing the cartridges as only the last in a series of acts which strained allegiance to the breaking. 'The English,' they said, 'are people who overthrow all religions.' In the army, it is true, the fear of religious defilement was universal, and the army knew its power. It held all the treasuries and most of the fortresses; and the European force was weak and dangerously reduced. But the fear had fallen also on the villages and the country people, and it was all the more potent and infectious from its vagueness. Panic spreads like wildfire among ignorant and superstitious people. On this inflammable material the too true story of the cartridges fell as a spark on dry tinder. The revolts at Meerut and Delhi were unchecked and unpunished. As one successful émeute occurred after another, the British Government seemed paralysed. Its authority was thrown off, and the Mutiny of the army assumed in places the character of a partial rebellion of the people already made uneasy by military revolt, innovation and change.

No long reflection was needed to see the tremendous import of what had taken place at Delhi. The most sanguine could feel no confidence as to how the country would go. At that moment there were in the Punjab about 58,000 trained Native soldiers all told. European troops had been massed in the Punjab, but they numbered only 10,500 men. They were broken up into two sections at the extreme ends of the province —one in the Pesháwar valley, and the other in the Simla Hills,—with weak detachments dotted at intervals between, at Firozpur, Jálandhar, Lahore, Siálkot, and Ráwal Pindi. Of the Native troops 36,000 belonged to the Bengal army, and not a man of them was to be trusted. The others, numbering over 20,000, were irregular troops and military police raised in the Punjab. Everything depended on how they would act. Should they make common cause with the Hindustáni army, our position was hopeless, and we were lost. If they stood true, we might weather the storm, we might save the province, we might save the Empire. What had we to offer them?

In this instance we could not play off the Muhammadan against the Hindu. Those fatal cartridges seemed to have been compounded with a Satanic ingenuity to create a common ground. If the fat of the cow excited the horror of the Bráhman Sepoy, the fat of swine was an abomination to the Muhammadan; and the Sepoys believed the cartridges to be smeared with both. Between the Sikh and the Muhammadan there was ancestral hatred. The Muhammadans had hunted the Sikhs like wild beasts, slain their priests with the sword, razed their holy temple and besprinkled the ruins with the blood of the cow. In the zenith of their power, the Sikhs stabled their horses in the mosques and turned the tombs of Muhammadan saints into pigsties. A true Sikh is damned if he place on his head anything belonging to a Muhammadan. He is required by his Bible to fight a Muhammadan face to face whenever he meets him. And yet, only a few years before, the Sikh and the Muhammadan had combined in an unnatural alliance and laid aside their national animosities in the common hatred of the English name. Manifestly there was little hope to be placed on antipathies of creed.

But now we were to reap the rich blessing of Lawrence's vigorous and beneficent rule. Not many years had passed since the country tasted to the full the bitterness of military tyranny. The memory of it was recent; the people were prosperous; there was no desire for its return. At the same time many looked upon the struggle before us as almost hopeless, and therefore displayed no eagerness to support the British rule. The people waited upon circumstance, and those early moments were precious moments. Fortunately Sir John Lawrence and his officers were men of nerve, fearless of responsibility, who knew how to take occasion by the hand,

> 'And if some dreadful deed should rise
> Would strike, and firmly, and one stroke.'

Promptitude and decision turned the scale. On the 12th of May the terrible news of the disasters at Meerut and Delhi was received. Before twenty-four hours were over, the Native troops at Lahore, who were on the watch for the signal from below, were disarmed, three thousand well-trained soldiers piling their arms, 'with silent and angry astonishment,' before some four hundred European infantry with twelve guns; the fort at Lahore was secured; the great magazine at Firozpur, containing upwards of seven thousand barrels of gunpowder and immense stores of arms, was saved; the fort of Govindgarh, the key of the Mánjha which Ranjít Singh had made almost impregnable, was occupied; the arsenal at Phillaur with the siege train was transferred to the guard of European troops; and every District Officer was made alive to the magnitude of the crisis and warned to secure his treasure, to deal firmly with the first symptoms of disorder, but to be quiet and calm and show no sign of alarm or excitement. Nothing, said Sir John Lawrence, conduces more to overawe the Natives than a quiet, resolute demeanour. And so, all over the province, except for a short time in the Cis-Sutlej States, the work went on as if nothing were wrong.

No precaution was omitted to prevent the spread of the treasonable infection. A system of passports was introduced; guards at the ferries were doubled, with orders to prevent the passage of suspicious characters, especially fakírs and mendicants; letters addressed to mutinous regiments were opened; the Native Press was put under censorship; District Officers and their Assistants did nightly patrol work, and showed themselves more than ever in the remote parts of their Districts; every Officer had to be at his post, and no leave of absence was granted except for certified sickness. Pesháwar 'stood in a ring of repressed hostilities.' Here a Council of War assembled, of which the moving spirits were Herbert Edwardes, John Nicholson, and Sydney Cotton who commanded the troops. In communication with Sir John Lawrence at Ráwal Pindi, measures were at once planned for the preservation of order. Here was devised, on Nicholson's initiative, the famous Movable Column of picked men, European and Punjabi, to patrol the country and swoop down on mutiny at the first signal of alarm. It was destined to execute terrible vengeance upon revolted Sepoys and in due time to be the last bolt which Sir John Lawrence was to hurl against Delhi.

Self-reliance so calm and resolute, vigour so manly and so instantly displayed, showed the vitality of our cause and drew to our side the languid current of popular support. By the 17th of May it became manifest that the rebels would receive no help from the people of the Punjab. The bold measures taken at Lahore on the morning of the 13th of May by Montgomery and Corbett, quieted the Sikhs of the Mánjha and secured for us Amritsar on which the loyalty of the Khálsa depended. At Pesháwar the leading men held aloof and watched events. 'If Pesháwar holds firm,' said a sagacious old Native[1], 'it is well; otherwise—' and he rolled up the skirt of his muslin robe significantly between his finger and his thumb. When the enlistments at Pesháwar first began, not a hundred men could be found to join our cause. On the morning of the 22nd of May the Bengal troops were to be deprived of their arms. 'As we rode to the disarming,' says Sir Herbert Edwardes[2], 'a very few chiefs and yeomen of the

[1] *The Crisis in the Punjab*, p. 33.

[2] *Life*, vol. ii. p. 133.

country attended us; and I remember judging from their faces that they came to see which way the tide would turn. As we rode back, friends were as thick as summer flies; and levies began from that moment to come in.' The Málikdín Afrídís were at the time under a ban for the murder of a Police Officer. Not long afterwards, a party of three hundred of them marched into cantonments, armed to the teeth, to fight for us, and begged to be forgiven. They formed the nucleus of one of the new Punjab regiments.

It is remarkable that the Muhammadans, especially the Border Patháns, Edwardes' old men, were the first to flock to our standard. They were rigid Mussalmáns, 'who never missed a prayer, and many of whom rode with the Korán at their saddle-bow.' Sikhs enlisted, but not in great numbers. They held back until Delhi had fallen, and then recruits came in thousands from the Mánjha. The bankers and the moneyed classes too played a trimming part. Money was urgently needed as well as soldiers. A six per cent. loan of £1,000,000 was put out, but only £420,000 was taken up, of which one-third was subscribed by the Ruling Chiefs who had already thrown in their lot with us. In the wealthy cities of Lahore and Amritsar, it is said in the official papers of the day that men worth half a million sterling offered a subscription of a hundred pounds, and others on the same scale. During the crisis the securities of the local loan fell as low as twenty-six per cent. discount, affording 'a good barometer of the state of the feeling towards us entertained by the moneyed classes in the province.'

Next to Pesháwar perhaps the greatest danger was to be feared in the Cis-Sutlej States. I have already narrated how these Chiefs were taken under British protection and maintained in their sovereign rights. The number of Chiefships was legion, and they varied in size and importance from large and powerful States like Patiála 'to the pettiest lordship or barony consisting of the tenth or twentieth share in a single village.' Nowhere in all India had the British claim to escheats been more systematically enforced. Up to the time of the Mutiny nineteen Chiefships, covering an area of 811 square miles and yielding an annual revenue of £45,000 had thus lapsed by the failure of direct heirs. After the First Sikh War, an area of 2,774 square miles and a revenue of £75,000 were confiscated for failure in duty on the part of the Chiefs. And after the Second War all the Chiefs, with nine exceptions, were reduced to the position of ordinary British subjects. Of the nine States excepted, two subsequently became escheats, and one was suppressed for misgovernment. In 1857 only six remained[1]. The elements of discontent among the influential families were therefore plentiful. Added to this, the population consists of Játs, Rájputs, Gujars, and other tribes allied to those in the Delhi

[1] These are Patiála, Jínd, Nábha, Máler-Kotla, Farídkot, and Kalsiá.

Territory, and, being close to the imperial city, they felt the first wave of insurrection.

Sir John Lawrence lost not a day in enlisting the active services of the Native Princes. Everything depended on getting them to declare themselves. Within a few hours after receiving the intelligence from Delhi, he wrote personally to the Ruling Chiefs and to many men of influence in the Punjab, that now was the time to prove their loyalty and earn a good name. And nobly they responded. The Rájá of Kapúrthala furnished a contingent of 2,000 men which took the place of the mutinied troops at Jálandhar and, headed by the Rájá in person, afterwards marched to Oudh and fought in six actions on our side. 'The Rájá of Jínd,' says the official report, 'was actually the first man, European or Native, who took the field against the mutineers. He openly declared at once that he should side with the British, under whom he had lived happily for fifty years—a speech calculated to give the right turn to Native opinion.' He marched with a contingent of 800 men to Karnál, and cleared the road as the British troops advanced upon Delhi. The Mahárájá of Patiála supplied 5,000 men, horse and foot; and held the line of communication between the Punjab and the army before Delhi for a distance of 120 miles. The contingent of the Rájá of Nábha, 800 strong, occupied the fort of Ludhiána, and escorted the siege train from Phillaur. The petty Sikh Chiefs complained of it as a grievance if they were not called on for help. Of all the Ruling Chiefs under the control of the Punjab Government, two only, one of them a petty hill Chieftain, failed in their duty. Well might the heart of Lord Canning warm within him when, after peace was restored, he found himself welcomed in the midst of these Chiefs. 'In other parts of India,' he said, as he addressed them at Lahore, 'I have received many distinguished Chiefs of ancient lineage who have proved themselves faithful feudatories of the Crown, and many of lower degree who have been dutiful subjects in the midst of great discouragements and dangers. But in the Punjab I find a whole nation of brave and loyal men.'

But although courage and self-reliance might serve to turn the tide of opinion for a time, the effect could not last unless Delhi were retaken. Sir John Lawrence saw at once the tremendous issues at stake. 'I consider this,' he wrote to the Commander-in-Chief, on the 13th of May, 'to be the greatest crisis which has ever occurred in India.' He knew the prestige of Delhi and the spell of the imperial name. Till Delhi was recovered nothing was secure; if Delhi should hold out long, all was lost. The rebellion could not be slain except by a blow at the heart. Delhi was not within Lawrence's province. It was a hundred miles beyond his frontier. But his vision was imperial. The struggle was for the supremacy of India, not for the safety of the Punjab. The Punjab could not stand if the Empire fell. Every nerve must be strained to the breaking to recover Delhi. The

European force was small, dangerously small; but the resources of England were inexhaustible and reinforcements would come in time. Providentially, the Persian war was over and the troops were returning, bringing Outram and Havelock. Then there was the China force, to divert which to India seems to have occurred at once to many master-minds—to Lord Canning, to Sir John Lawrence, to his brother Henry, to Sir Patrick Grant, to General Hearsey. Fortunately Lord Elgin was a statesman who could realise the supreme need, and who shrank not from the responsibility of yielding to Lord Canning's call. Meanwhile there were the regiments in the Simla Hills. These should go down by forced marches, and on the back of them should be poured the Punjab troops, the contingents of the loyal Chiefs and every man the province could spare. The season of the year was deadly to the European soldier; but elephants and Native gigs and camels would carry the foot-sore and weary; a pony between two would enable them to make double marches and to walk and ride alternately.

Not a day was to be lost; time was everything. The Chief Commissioner remembered the success of his own rapid strokes when Kángra rose. He remembered how the delay before Múltán had changed a local émeute into the rebellion of the whole Sikh nation. 'Delay,' he knew, 'was only a less misfortune than a repulse.' It would bring thousands to the rebel standard. One vigorous stroke might disperse the mutineers before they gathered strength. The first success would encourage the faithful, decide the wavering and dishearten the evil-disposed. 'Pray, only reflect on the whole history of India,' he wrote again to the Commander-in-Chief. 'Where have we failed when we acted vigorously? Where have we succeeded when guided by timid counsels?' A common responsibility for the salvation of the Empire rested upon all. It was no time to stand on ceremony. Camels, coolies, carts, bullocks, were collected from every quarter. The country and the loyal Chiefs were put under requisition. And on the 17th of May, a week from the outbreak, the avenging force began to move forward from Ambála. Joining with the troops from Meerut, who fought two successful battles on the way, the united force was at Badlí-kí-Sarái, six miles from Delhi, on the 8th of June; defeated the mutineers; drove them back into the city; and occupied the Ridge which, with an open rear and exposed flanks, was to be the scene of heroic daring and patient endurance for the next four months.

It was a small force—barely 3,800 men all told. Some have thought that a rush on the city then and there would have put it in our hands. Military critics will form their opinion on data wider and more detailed than can be cited in a little book like this. But a rush from Meerut on the 11th of May would have been one thing; an assault on the 8th of June was another. The men were exhausted by battle and march; the defences of the city were seven miles in circumference; inside the walls would have been street-fighting with every advantage of numbers, cover, and local knowledge on the side of the mutineers; the small force would have been lost in the great city; failure meant the loss of the Empire. The enemy, it is true, had not yet been strongly re-inforced; but though defeated, they were not dispirited. On the 10th of June the Rchtak mutineers marched in, undeterred by the news of our three victories. In the pride of power every one underrated the strength of Delhi. Sir John Lawrence did not expect much resistance. His impression was that, on the approach of our troops, the mutineers would disperse or the citizens would rise and open their gates. Many believed that one battle would decide the fate of the place. Re-inforcements, as they came down, feared they might arrive too late to share in the assault. But Native opinion made a truer estimate; it was not till the spoils of Delhi began to pass up through the Punjab that the country believed the city to have fallen.

Every eye at Delhi was turned to Meerut through that fatal 11th of May. All through the early morning help had been looked for by the doomed victims at the fort. All through the long day Willoughby and his brave comrades maintained their despairing hold on the magazine. At the main guard the Sepoys were held to a wavering allegiance. From the cantonments and the Flag-staff Tower the eyes of women and children strained to catch sight of the expected relief.

Even the King could not believe that there was no pursuit. He sent out a rider on a camel along the Meerut road who returned with the report that there were no European troops within twenty miles[1]. The evening settled down on pillage and massacre, and there was no avenging hand. The green flag of Muhammad was hoisted on the minaret of the Great Mosque. With salute of guns and beat of drum the restoration of the Mughal rule was proclaimed. Next day a silver throne, on which the King used to sit to receive the homage of the representative of the Governor-General, but which he had put aside when this honour ceased to be paid to him, was brought from its recess into the Hall of Audience. The King took his seat upon it. The officers of our revolted Sepoys passed before him, one by one, and as they bowed the King put his hand on their head in acceptance of their allegiance. At the request of the soldiers Mírzá Mughal, one of the royal Princes, was made Commander-in-Chief, and other Princes were made colonels of regiments. A grand feast was given to the whole army. On the 16th of May, forty-nine Christian captives, nearly all of them women and children, were butchered in the palace. From that day no white face was seen in the city, neither was there any vestige or symbol of the rule that had been, save the uniforms and arms of the rebel troops, and the flutes and clarionets and drums of the five regimental

[1] *History of the Siege of Delhi*, by an Officer who served there, p. 39.

bands which daily played English music before the King.

Every day the King held court, and his proceedings, his health, his receptions, his siesta, his cooling drinks and the delicacies of his table, were reported for the edification of the public. But it was only royal state in name; the King was a puppet in the hands of the army. Orders were brought to him ready written out for his signature. He made a feeble attempt to assert himself, but his orders were set at nought. The cavalry stabled their horses in the royal gardens, and gallopped about within the precincts of the palace, even up to the Hall of Audience, places which, as the King pathetically complained, 'not even Nádir Sháh nor Ahmad Sháh, nor any of the British Governor-Generals of India ever entered on horseback.' The soldiers turned the palace buildings into barracks, neglected to salute, appeared before the King without their turbans, and even crowded into the Hall of Devotion with their shoes on. The shops of the merchants were broken open and plundered by the soldiers, headed sometimes by the Princes. The ruffians of the city put on the uniforms of Sepoys that they might plunder with greater impunity. Any pretext sufficed—a search for Europeans, a forced loan—or no pretext at all. The King's own seal was stolen, and an attempt was made to break into the apartments of the Queen. Even the men at the ice-pits who supplied the royal table were plundered, and the tinker who tinned 'the culinary vessels and other articles of the royal household' was not spared. The King himself in an address to the army described the sack and plunder as worse than that of Nádir Sháh, and the people complained that they 'had a foretaste of the day of judgment.' His orders despised, and his commands set at nought, the King had recourse to conciliation and entreaty. He appealed to his soldiers as his children, and prayed them to have respect to his old age and infirmities. It was all unavailing. And at last, wearied out by anarchy which he was powerless to control, the Shelter of the World, the Monarch of the 'royal court at which Darius might have served as a door-keeper,' begged that he might be allowed to retire to Mecca, and spend his few remaining days in devotion.

It is not easy to estimate the force against which we had to contend at Delhi. On the 11th of May there were of trained soldiers at least the King's own troops, the five regiments of infantry, the cavalry, and the artillery that composed the Native garrisons at Meerut and Delhi. By the end of May the whole of Rohilkhand was up, and by the middle of June every station in Oudh was in revolt. Two days after our handful of troops encamped on the Ridge, the rebels streamed in from Rohtak, and thereafter regiment after regiment, as it mutinied, from Jálandhar, from Nasírábád, from Bareilly, from Nímach, made for the imperial city. Towards the end of the siege, in an address to the Bombay army, the rebel leaders estimated their force at 'nearly 80,000 or 90,000 regular organised military troops,' besides 'nearly 10,000 or 15,000 regular and other cavalry.' About half the number would probably be nearer the truth. Writing about the same time, General Wilson estimated the garrison at full 40,000 soldiers armed and disciplined by ourselves, with 114 heavy pieces of artillery mounted on the walls, besides some 60 pieces of field artillery all of our own manufacture and manned by artillerymen drilled and taught by ourselves. By the end of July, with the accession of the Nímach brigade, the strength of the enemy was probably at its maximum. No more regiments remained to mutiny.

Sir John Lawrence made superhuman efforts to re-inforce the little army before Delhi. First to arrive were the famous Guides. They owed their origin to Sir Henry Lawrence. The characteristic features of this distinguished corps, as Edwardes observes [1], do not strike us now-a-days. 'But in 1846, to set Poorbeahs aside and to raise a corps of sharp-shooters or sportsmen of all nations, and say they should wear their own clothes and be hampered with as few accoutrements as possible, that they should have loose, dusky shirts instead of tight red jackets, sun-proof turbans instead of sunstroke Glengarry caps, and wide pijamas instead of pantaloons and straps and braces,—a change like that was literally a stroke of genius. It was an invention.' Starting from Mardán on the 13th

[1] *Life*, vol. ii. p. 108.

of May six hours after they got their orders, the Guides, under command of Captain Henry Daly, reached Delhi on the 9th of June, covering 580 miles in twenty-two marches with three intervening halts. It was the hottest season of the year, and the rate of marching could not have been performed by the infantry on foot. But a camel was allowed to every two men which enabled them to keep up with the cavalry, and to get over thirty or forty miles between sunset and sunrise. They marched into camp as light of step as if coming off parade, and three hours after arrival they engaged the enemy in a fight, in which the Second in Command was killed, and two other Officers were wounded. During the four months of the siege these magnificent soldiers were constantly in action, sometimes twice a day, and out of 800 men 350 were killed and wounded.

By the beginning of July the besieging force amounted to 6,600 men—quite enough to beat the rebels in the open field; but it had made no impression on the city. Not a single gun of the enemy had been silenced. The siege train that had been sent from Phillaur was altogether too weak. Our fire was returned four shots to one, with a precision which showed that the enemy had got the exact range of every point of the camp. We had by that time been engaged in ten fights, in seven of which the whole force was employed. In every one we were victorious, but the capture of the city was as far off as ever. It was the policy of the enemy to wear us out. False alarms served this purpose as well as regular attacks, for the men had to turn out and got no rest. They chose the hottest hours for their assaults, when the sun in its course fought against us. Twice an escalade was arranged for and abandoned. It was too desperate a risk. Our losses were very heavy. In one week twenty-five Officers and 400 men were killed or wounded. Ague, fever, dysentery, sunstroke, and cholera too were doing their fatal work. 'A regiment which had come in 600 strong was in three weeks brought down to 242 out of hospital[1].' At this rate the annihilation of the little British force was an easy calculation. Matters at Delhi began to look very serious. Withdrawal was gravely considered and was openly discussed at the mess-tables. It was obvious to all that Delhi could not be taken without large re-inforcements.

[1] *History of the Siege of Delhi*, p. 232.

CHAPTER VI

THE MUTINY (*continued*)

THE long and unexpected resistance of Delhi began to work evil in the Punjab. When the avenging force was despatched from Ambála, there remained only about 7,500 European troops to watch 33,000 Hindustáni soldiers. The disarmaments at Lahore on the 13th of May, Peshåwar on 22nd, Nowshera on 26th, and Múltán on the 10th of June, made the work easier, while the annihilation of the mutineers at Mardán on the 21st of May covered the feebleness with which the Sepoys were dealt with at Firozpur and Jálandhar. There was no more trouble all through June. But as the season wore on, more Europeans had to be sent to Delhi, and sickness so reduced the rest that not more than 4,700 were left effective to watch 18,000 men, of whom 6,000 were armed. Still Delhi held out. And then again Mutiny began to raise its head. On the 7th of July the Sepoys rose at Jehlam; nearly all were captured or destroyed. On the 9th there was Mutiny with murder at Siálkot: the rebels were intercepted by Nicholson and destroyed. On the 30th there was Mutiny with murder at Lahore: the mutineers were destroyed to the last man. Evidently the English government was not yet doomed.

Still the outlook was very gloomy. Everywhere from below Delhi came reports of the disappearance of the British power. Many began to doubt; some began to trim. Even the brave heart of Lawrence almost failed him. For a whole month he feared we should not weather the storm. Our salvation lay in the speedy fall of Delhi. The battle was to be won or lost at Delhi and nowhere else. 'Recollect,' he wrote on the 24th of July, 'if you fall back from Delhi, our cause is gone; neither the Punjab nor anything else can stand.' Delhi must be taken at every cost. It was the crisis of our fate. Then it was that Sir John Lawrence made his last and boldest venture. He issued letters (July 23rd) to the Sikh Chiefs calling upon them to furnish troopers from the old Sikh army, and he wound up with the significant words, 'I would not put up with any delay or hesitation on your part.' He hurled at Delhi the Movable Column. The last available European was sent. A corps of Mazhabí[1] Sikhs, 1,200 strong, was raised at the suggestion of Edwardes from the workmen on the canals, to serve as sappers and miners. Old Sikh artillerymen, who could strip their sleeves and show the scars received in honourable fight against

[1] Descendants of the sweepers whom Guru Govind sent to Delhi to fetch the body of his martyred father and whom he received into the Khálsa for their daring courage. *Mazhabí* is from the Arabic and means *regular due* Sikhs. Trumpp, lxxxviii.

us, were enlisted and sent down to serve in the trenches.

On the 4th of September, the heavy siege train from Firozpur, drawn by sixteen elephants, and 548 country waggons, with stores of ammunition, 'sufficient it was said to grind Delhi to powder,' entered camp. On the 6th came a remnant of Europeans from Meerut, who had been relieved by levies from the Punjab. On the 8th the Kashmír contingent, 2,000 strong with 200 cavalry and 6 guns, arrived. It was now the beginning of the end for the enemy or for us. 'We have sent,' wrote Sir John to Lord Canning, 'every man we could spare, perhaps more.' 'I have sent all I can, perhaps more than I ought to have sent.' Edwardes from Pesháwar, becoming alarmed for the safety of the Punjab, on which the fate of the Empire depended, had long before entreated him not to be engulfed in Delhi. 'Delhi is not India.' 'Don't let yourself be sucked to death by inches.' The position of the Punjab was now critical indeed, as was shown by the defeated conspiracy in Lower Hazára, and by the rising at Gugera on the very evening of the assault on Delhi—émeutes arising from no discontent, but from a belief that the knell of the British power had rung.

The sequel is soon told. Everything was now ready for the final trial of strength. In the city the enemy began to see that the days of the short-lived Mughal triumph were numbered. Reproaches, dissensions, and mutual recriminations divided the rebels, now depressed by constant defeat in more than thirty fights. Women and children began to leave the city.

Twice the King made ineffectual overtures for capitulation. On the night of the 7th of September the first breaching battery was silently traced out. By the 13th of September the breaches were reported ready for the assault. Before daybreak on the 14th of September, the same day on which the King's ancestor Sháh Alam had been delivered by us from the thraldom of the Maráthás fifty-four years before, the assault was delivered. On the 16th the magazine was taken with over 170 pieces of ordnance and immense stores almost unaffected by the great explosion and the drain of the siege. On the 20th the British flag was hoisted on the royal palace, and the whole city was in the possession of the British troops. The story of the King's capture and the slaughter of the three Princes by Hodson is well known. In the Hall of Audience, where he had held mimic court, the aged King was brought to trial on the 27th of January, 1858, on charges of rebellion, treason, and murder. On the 9th of March he was found guilty and sentenced to perpetual exile. He was removed to Rangoon, where he died on the 7th of November, 1862. No weekly lamp is lit on Thursdays at his tomb. No verse from the Korán is inscribed over him. His grave is probably now unknown to any living man. So perished the Mughal name.

The effect of the fall of Delhi was instantaneous. It was felt in the remotest corner of the province.

It was felt in Afghánistán, where, as Lumsden tells us [1], the excitement 'entirely subsided on the fall of Delhi.' Pesháwar was illuminated for several nights in succession. From sunset to sunrise the city was brilliant with lamps and fireworks. Six per cent. paper which had fallen to 26 per cent. discount rose rapidly to par. Rich merchants began to apologise for not having subscribed to the loan. Fair-weather friends came to the front with their congratulations. Our prestige stood higher than ever. Soon the spoils of Delhi, which had been given over to three days' plunder, began to pass up and to be seen in the villages. The Sikhs of the Mánjha, who had been waiting like eagles with trimmed and quivering wing, now began to gather to the carcass. Many villages were 'almost decimated by the number of recruits' who crowded to the new regiments. We had weathered the gale. The Mutiny at Miánwáli and other little incidents were only the last ripples of the expiring storm. So calm did the atmosphere become that, within three months after the fall of Delhi, as many as seven hundred new village schools were founded in the Punjab.

But this was only a breathing time. Below Delhi every trace of English dominion had in many Districts been wiped out, and the country had to be reconquered. From Delhi the pursuit lingered, so that the mutineers escaped and disappeared in the seething rebellion below. Nicholson, as he lay dying of his

[1] *The Mission to Kandahár*, para. 9.

wound, vexed his impatient soul because of the delay. But the troops were too exhausted by the assault and a week of street-fighting for immediate pursuit. Not till the 24th of September could the column move. The Native portion of it was all Punjabi. After them regiment upon regiment was marched down from the Punjab to the aid of the Commander-in-Chief as fast as they could be raised. Recruits appeared as if by magic. Altogether it is estimated that at one time there were upwards of 70,000 disciplined Punjabis under arms, of whom about 23,000 were employed beyond the limits of the province. About one-third of the new army were Sikhs; the rest belonged to various races of Hindus, hillmen from Kángra and Jammu, and Muhammadans from the Punjab and beyond the border, differing in race, language, and customs, and 'having little in common except religion.'

The effect of this wholesale enlistment on the peace of the Punjab was very marked. Never had the frontier been so quiet. The new regiments absorbed all the ruffians of the Peshâwar valley. 'Indeed,' says Sir Herbert Edwardes, 'it must be admitted that one troop alone, that is now fighting at Lucknow, contains no less than sixty outlaws headed by the redoubted Mukarram Khán. These men had harried our border for years, and would undoubtedly have rioted in this hour of our weakness, if not suddenly put in the way of an honest livelihood. As the Native gentleman who raised the troop remarked,

"Whether they kill the Poorbeahs or the Poorbeahs kill them, it will be an equal service to the State!"'

Exclusive reliance on the Punjab as a recruiting ground was unavoidable at the time. All the rest of Upper India was lost to us. But Lawrence was fully aware of the danger of it. 'It strikes me,' he wrote to Sir Colin Campbell, 'that there is some danger that our Officers, in their horror of John Pandy, may go into the other extreme and make too much of John Singh. We can no more rest our trust on the Punjabi than on the Hindustani!' He greatly feared lest the Punjabis should see and feel their strength. The faithful chief of Patiála saw the danger, and raised his warning voice. Nothing was to be feared while the war lasted. Excitement of battle and lust of plunder left no room for disloyal intrigues; but 'wait,' he said, 'till you mass large bodies of Sikhs in your cantonments, and then remember that I warned you of the danger.' In the reconstruction of the Bengal army this difficulty has been wisely solved. Including the Frontier Force, it numbers in all 74,000 men of mixed races and religion. There are 39,000 from the Punjab and the frontier tribes which border it; and of these 19,000 are Sikhs.

Certainly no troops ever fought more bravely or covered themselves with more glory than did the Punjab troops in our cause against the rebel Sepoys. They shared with us the privations and diseases and dangers of the Ridge, 'soldier all day and sentinel all through the night.' They shared the glory of the assault. In the Oudh and Rohilkhand campaign they were shoulder to shoulder with the best and the bravest. They have sustained their reputation in many a hard fought field since then. And what is more, there has sprung up in the Punjab a feeling of brotherhood to England and of loyalty to the Crown which it will be our own fault if we alienate. In the spring of 1885, when war with Russia was imminent, and preparations were begun for an expected campaign, many of the war-worn veterans of the Mutiny days came—with white hair and bent with the weight of years—to the present writer and laid their swords at his feet, recounting the favours and honours they had received, and begging, though too old and battered to go themselves, that their sons might not be forgotten when the roll for service was called.

Delhi after the capture became like a city of the dead. Not an inhabitant remained. An eye-witness describing it says that for miles not a creature was to be seen save a half-starved cat, and here and there a withered hag groping about among the old papers and rags with which the city was strewn. The European artillery were quartered in the Arabic college. The Great Mosque, one of the finest works of the reign of Sháh Jahán, unsurpassed in beauty by any building of the kind in India, became a barrack for the Sikhs. Military law was proclaimed, and a military governor appointed. The houses of the leaders and active participators in the rebellion were confiscated. Within a few days after our occupation, Sir John Lawrence was desirous to let the people return to the city as soon as military arrangements for the security of the palace could be completed. He was moved by the sufferings of the multitude, nine-tenths of whom had taken no active share in the outbreak. But other views prevailed. Hindus were allowed after a time gradually to come back to their homes. The Muhammadan population was altogether excluded. In May, 1858, it was estimated that the population did not amount to one-fourth of its former number. Not till 1859 was the attachment taken off the houses of the Muhammadans, and the order for their exclusion removed.

Of course it was necessary to make a severe example of mutineers and all who were guilty of the shedding of blood. Rebellion had to be crushed remorselessly; and that could not be done without blood. Severity in the beginning was seen to be mercy in the end. 'The sooner blood be let,' said Edwardes, 'the less of it will suffice.' Sir John Lawrence's grip upon the mutineers was relentless. For ringleaders and murderers there was no mercy; and till Delhi was taken,—so long, that is, as the fate of the country hung in a trembling balance which a straw might turn, so long his hand was pitiless. He would open with grape upon insurgents who broke into mutiny. He would raise the hue and cry against them; he would rouse the country by offer of rewards for their capture; he would hunt them down as Thags and Dakáits had been hunted down. But this was in no wantonness of severity. To spare guilty blood meant that more innocent blood would be shed. But if Lawrence was very stern, he was never vindictive. First to strike, he was the first to stay his hand. He was the first to recommend the promise of life to those who had not committed murder and would throw down their arms. He objected to the execution without mercy of all the prisoners of the 55th N. I., though taken fighting against us; and he saved the lives of two-thirds of them by what the military authorities considered a misplaced humanity. When the Gugera insurrection was put down, he begged his officers not to be too severe. 'You can try and punish capitally a few of the ring-leaders,' he wrote; 'don't hang too many.'

Lawrence was much moved by the excesses of the Prize Agents in Delhi and did all in his power, both by the telegraph and by letter, to put a stop to acts which, in his opinion, reflected disgrace on our national honour. He recommended that Delhi should be freed from martial law. However guilty some of its inhabitants may have been, the majority had no connection with the rebellion. Many indeed would have sided with us if they had been able. The destruction of the city and its noble buildings was repugnant alike to his reason and his feelings. 'I will on no account consent to it,' was his answer to a proposal to level the Great Mosque with the ground; 'there are many things you could persuade me to do, but you shall never persuade me to do this; so you may as well spare your pains.'

While dealing severely with the principals in rebellion and murder, he insisted on leniency to the many and a fair trial to all. A war of extermination would be cruel injustice. Multitudes had been coerced into insurrection by the force of circumstances, and had only shifted for themselves when we were no longer able to protect them. These would quietly settle down if they got a chance. So long as we classed all mutineers and rebels together, with no distinction of degrees of guilt, so long would they hold together; the country would never be pacified; and the people, getting inured to a life of rapine and lawlessness, would fall back into a worse condition than that from which we had rescued them. Dealing destruction with one hand, we should hold out the olive-branch of peace with the other. A place of repentance given would sow distrust among the rebels and divide their ranks. It would show the world we had some feelings of mercy. Above all, it was demanded by the mercy which God had shown to us. 'There is a judge over both them and us[1]. Inasmuch as we have been preserved from impending destruction by His mercy alone, we should be merciful to others: reflecting that, if He were to be extreme to mark what we have done and still do amiss, we should forfeit that protection from on High, which alone

[1] Letter to Government of India forwarding the Mutiny Report, No. 75, dated 25th May, 1858, para. 21.

maintains us in India.' Therefore he pleaded for an amnesty to those who, not being guilty of blood, should throw down their arms and quietly go to their homes.

It is difficult now, even for those who lived through it all, to realise the terrible ferocity of vengeance that swelled in the English breast, or to appreciate how much excuse there was for it. There was not a home in Upper India which the bullet or the sword of the Sepoy had not reached. Many hearts were torn by the foul and treacherous murder of those dearest to them; all mourned the loss of friends, slain sometimes under circumstances of diabolical cruelty. The perfidy and blood-thirstiness which in some places attended the outbreak inflamed every bad and bitter passion and stirred, even in the hearts of gentle women, a desire for indiscriminate vengeance. Many clamoured for the destruction of Delhi; raze it, raze it, even to the foundations thereof. A more moderate proposal, which found much favour at the time, was to convert the Great Mosque into a Christian church, and on each of the thousand compartments of its marble floor to inscribe the name of one of the Christian martyrs of the Mutiny. To restore the building to the Muhammadans was scouted as madness. An officer of the Government drew on himself the wrath of the newspapers because he took off his hat when he went into the chamber where the old King was kept a prisoner. Such was the excitement of the time that the judgment of the wisest and calmest was carried away, and even the brave became sometimes cruel. The provocation was unexampled, and who will dare to judge? The very Legislature was infected. Ferocious laws were passed; yet England did not raise her voice.

Persons convicted of mutiny, desertion, rebellion, or waging war against the Government, of seducing soldiers from their allegiance, or of exciting them to mutiny or sedition, were made liable to the punishment of death and forfeiture of property. In Districts where martial law was proclaimed, it was death to commit or attempt to commit any crime whatever with the intention of assisting those who were waging war against the State or of forwarding their designs. In those Districts, also, any heinous offence was punishable with death: and a heinous offence was so defined as to include crimes ranging from murder to the destruction of property provided for the conveyance or subsistence of troops, to entering a dwelling-house and stealing therein, and even to receiving property obtained by burglary. Sepoys were liable to be tatooed on the left side with letters an inch long, branding them as mutineers or deserters, and so made as to be conspicuous and not liable to be obliterated. Offences might be tried by any person invested with the powers of a Sessions Judge, or by a Commission issued by the Government or by any person whom the Governor-General in Council might authorise to issue it. There was no appeal. Sentences were final, and the penalty of death might be executed immediately on conviction. The terrible vengeance executed under these Draconian laws is matter of history[1].

As soon as the first wave of excitement had passed away, Lawrence did all he could to mitigate their severity. Delhi, as I have explained, was outside his jurisdiction. No civil authority was yet established there. But it was impossible to govern the country from below through an intervening belt of rebellion, and circumstances threw it into his hands. The condition of the city and the reckless proceedings of the Special Commissioners had long been causing him deep anxiety. In the end of January, 1858, he set out for Delhi. Immediately on his arrival he telegraphed to Lord Canning and begged that the power of sentencing men to death might be withdrawn from Officers acting alone and without colleagues. He

[1] In the Administration Report for 1856-7 and 1857-8 the following returns of the proceedings of the Special Commissioners in the Punjab are given :—

	By military tribunals.	*By Civil Authorities.*	*Total.*
Sentenced to death :			
Hanged	86	300	386
Shot	628	1,370	1,998
Imprisoned	245	1,226	1,471
Flogged	—	1,501	1,501
Total punished ...	959	4,397	5,356

Nearly half (2,025) were convicted by the Special Commissioners at Delhi.

appointed a Commission of Three to try State offences and required that the Commissioners should sit together in all cases calling for a severer punishment than three years' imprisonment. He directed that in every case the evidence and the defence should be recorded, and that weekly returns of all cases tried should be submitted to him. These measures gave great satisfaction and did much to restore the confidence of the Natives and bring them back to the city.

Meantime, the Districts round Delhi had been pacified. Early in the Mutiny a force of new levies hurriedly collected, with detachments of police and some troops supplied by the Chiefs of Bikaner and Patiála, had been sent under General Van Cortlandt, to recover the Districts to the West. Disorder had necessarily followed the collapse of British authority. In Rohtak and Gurgáon anarchy reigned unchecked. Gujars and Meos plundered with impartial hand, respecting the King's government no more than our own. Convoys of his treasure were attacked; the Delhi King's officers were robbed and beaten; and his letters were torn into fragments and thrown in the face of his messengers. Old feuds, some of which had lain dormant since the days of the Mughal Emperors, were revived and fought out. The country people however bore the English no special ill-will, and as soon as Delhi fell, the Districts rapidly settled down. In the Delhi District for instance, the revenue due in June, 1857, was collected in part, and that due in

December was paid in full. The civil administration was re-established and superintended from Lahore. By a resolution of the Government of India dated the 9th of February, 1858, and by a subsequent enactment, the Delhi Territory was formally separated from the North-Western Provinces and attached to the Punjab under the administration of Sir John Lawrence. The territory thus added to the Punjab contains, according to the most recent statistics, an area of 12,674 square miles, and a population of 3,357,817 souls. It yields a land-revenue of about £275,000 and a revenue from all sources of £350,000.

CHAPTER VII

From Chief Commissioner to Viceroy

And now the time was approaching for well-earned and honoured repose. Lawrence's wife and family had gone to England in December 1857, but he felt bound to stay one year more till order should be completely restored. Having put things right at Delhi, he returned to Lahore and retreated to Murree when the summer heat began. From there he submitted to the Government of India a report on the events of 1857 and his recommendations for the reward of all who had done loyal service in the dark and cloudy day. As a rule Sir John Lawrence was sparing in his acknowledgment of services and seldom praised a man to his face. But he never forgot good work or missed a chance of pushing forward those who did their duty with zeal and intelligence. And sometimes his feelings would burst out in a gush of generous emotion. 'Your Lahore men have done nobly,' he wrote to Montgomery after the disarming of Meean Meer, 'I should like to embrace them.' And to Nicholson after Najafgarh, 'I wish I had the power of knighting you on the spot.' He took to himself little credit.

'Next to the indomitable valour of the European soldiery,' he wrote to Edwardes, 'the Punjabis, white and black, have done the deed. I however look upon myself as only one of them. Few men in a similar position have had so many good and true supporters around him. But for them what could I have done?' But for all that, history confirms the verdict of Edward Thornton—'Looking back now on all that happened, I can see clearly that it was he and none of his subordinates who can be said to have saved the Punjab.' Or as Edwardes puts it—'Any treatment of the picture, therefore, that would put John in other than the first place would be thoroughly untrue.' 'Through him Delhi fell,' was the verdict of Lord Canning, 'and the Punjab, no longer a weakness, became a source of strength. But for him, the hold of England over Upper India would have had to be recovered at a cost of English blood and treasure which defies calculation.'

Leaving Murree in October, 1858, Lawrence paid a last visit to Pesháwar, where he read out to the paraded troops the Queen's Proclamation transferring the Government of India from the East India Company to the Crown; and proclaiming mercy to all offenders in the Mutiny save and except those convicted of taking part in the murder of British subjects. The royal clemency caused general rejoicing, and all hearts were thankful to God that the day of retributive justice was over, and the torrent of blood had at last ceased to flow. This Proclamation is the Charter of the rights of the people and the Princes of India. Returning to Lahore, Sir John Lawrence made preparations for his deparature. In the meantime honours had been showered upon him. He was made a Knight Grand Cross of the Bath, a Baronet, and a Privy Councillor. The freedom of the City of London was voted him, and the Court of Directors granted him a special annuity of £2000. Sir Colin Campbell thought he should have got a peerage, and some dissatisfaction was caused in England by its being withheld. But Lawrence was too much of a philosopher to vex himself. He had, he said, lived long enough and seen sufficient to teach him that 'the best reward any man can have is the feeling that he has done his duty to the best of his ability.'

On the 1st of January, 1859, the territories under his administration were constituted a Lieutenant-Governorship, and on the same date, as was fitting, the *Gazette* announced that 'the Right Honourable the Viceroy and Governor-General of India has been pleased to appoint the Honourable Sir John Lawrence, Baronet, G.C.B., to be the first Lieutenant-Governor of the Punjab and its Dependencies.' Lord Dalhousie had proposed it three years before. But the Court of Directors thought the measure premature, and objected also on financial grounds. In the end of 1858 Lord Stanley re-opened the question and, pending the discussion and settlement of it, Sir John Lawrence was granted the salary and establishment of a Lieutenant-Governor. But the arrangement came too late to be of much service to him either in emoluments or in relief from work. He left Lahore on February 26th, 1859, to join his family in England. No one who was present at the parting is ever likely to forget it. We all assembled, soldiers and civilians, clergy and laity, Natives and Europeans, in the old Native tomb which did, and still does, duty for a Government House at Lahore, to bid him an affectionate farewell, and presented to him an address which was read by Mr. Macleod, afterwards Sir Donald and Lieutenant-Governor. Few of us looked unmoved on the strong face furrowed by care and sickness, or on the once stalwart frame worn with long service and broken by the anxiety of the crisis through which India had passed. His mantle fell on the worthy shoulders of Montgomery, whose prevision in procuring the disarmament of the Native troops at Meean Meer on the eventful morning of May 13th, 1857, and whose cheerful courage and promptitude ever after throughout the Mutiny, have imperishably associated his name with the Punjab, second only to his great Chief. Sir John made over the government to his successor in profound peace. He was able to write to Lord Canning:—'The whole country, from end to end, is as quiet as possible. Indeed, I never recollect to have seen the people so loyal and contented.'

The events of the Mutiny profoundly stirred the deep religious nature of Sir John Lawrence. He had seen the British power in Upper India drowned in a deluge of blood. He had seen the Punjab saved as if by fire. In recounting the difficulties and dangers he had surmounted, he acknowledged that the first cause was the mercy of God. 'No doubt,' he said, 'humanly speaking, the Punjab possessed great advantages; . . . but as a protection against the peril of the time, all such advantages were as nothing without the support of the everlasting arm of Almighty God. To Him alone, therefore, be all the praise!' 'It was not policy,' wrote Montgomery—for there were many saintly men in the Punjab besides its Chief—'or soldiers, or officers, that saved the Indian Empire to England, and saved England to India. The Lord our God, He it was.' In Montgomery's expression of humble thankfulness, Sir John Lawrence devoutly joined:—'It is owing to an overruling Providence, and to that alone, that a single Englishman was left alive in the Punjab.'

It is not often that the guiding hand of God is so openly acknowledged in public documents. This Christian confession is not to be attributed to pious emotion excited by the solemnity of the time. Lawrence's religion was the moving power of his life, the mainspring of his single-hearted devotion to duty. No estimate of his life and work can be true that omits to take this into account. There was in him a strong spiritual force, working silently and unobtrusively, that leavened and moulded everything he did. Of him it may be said, as Carlyle wrote of Cromwell, to whom Lawrence has often been likened, that he 'believed in God, not on Sundays only, but on all days, in all places, and in all cases.' He never talked of his convictions, but it never entered into his honest mind to conceal them. His faith was simple, and he lived as he believed; so that his actions grounded themselves naturally on their religious basis. I have already noted how he begged for an amnesty to rebels in the spirit and almost in the words of the Lord's Prayer. His wife has told us that his faith was the most beautiful and simple she ever knew; fear God and keep His commandments was the rule of his daily life. 'We are told to pray and that our prayers will be answered, and that is sufficient for me,' he once said to his friend Captain Eastwick, when some one in his presence had objected to prayers for rain. When he turned the first sod of the first railway in the Punjab, on February 8th, 1859, prayers to God were offered up in the presence of the assembled Officers and Chiefs and a multitude of Natives, printed copies of the prayers having been distributed to the people beforehand.

With Lawrence the guiding policy in such questions was perfect toleration and complete religious liberty. He would as little brook encroachment on his own liberty of conscience as he would permit interference with the freedom of belief and religious worship of others. But in those days, strange as it may appear, the principles of religious liberty, in their application to servants of Government, seem to have been imperfectly understood. A few weeks after Sir John Lawrence had laid down the reins of office, the Government of India called the Commissioner of the Amritsar Division to account for attending the baptism of some adult Native converts in the private house of a Christian missionary. Of course the Commissioner vindicated himself by an unanswerable appeal to principles of religious liberty and to the Queen's Proclamation, claiming as a Christian official the same rights of private judgment and conduct as are allowed to Hindus and Muhammadans and Sikhs. Some three years later, in the Christmas of 1862, when a missionary conference was convened at Lahore, and was attended by many of the heroes of the Mutiny presided over by [Sir] Donald Macleod, there were some who would have put a stop to it as mischievous and not in keeping with official duty. Looked at in the light and practice of the present day, when officers of every degree take part in missionary meetings and conferences, and the highest in India, not omitting the Viceroy himself, lay the foundation stones of mission schools and churches, and acknowledge from the public platform the indebtedness of the Government to the Christian missionary, cases like those I have referred to provoke a smile of incredulity.

The revolution in Christian policy in India within the last quarter of a century has been complete. And not least among the causes which have brought about the change is the publication of the most famous and the most widely known of Sir John Lawrence's despatches—that of April 21st, 1858, on the doing of

Christian things in a Christian way. The circumstances are well known. Edwardes, as he pondered on the Mutiny, its causes and its lessons, came to the conclusion that the extent of suffering caused by the revolt proved it to be a divine chastisement for national sin in withholding Christian truth from the people. Under this conviction he wrote his celebrated paper on 'the elimination of all unchristian principles from the Government of India.' It was intended primarily to influence public opinion in England. Upon this memorandum Lawrence wrote his despatch, which, though stopping a long way short of Edwardes' proposals and on some points controverting his facts, was described by Edwardes himself as 'a fine manifesto' and 'a noble expression of the duty of the Indian Government to do whatever Christianity requires, at whatever cost.' After stating his views on the teaching of the Bible in Government schools and colleges—a religious instruction which Lawrence thought ought to be given wherever we have teachers fit to teach it, and pupils willing to hear it—on the endowment of Native religions, caste, the recognition of Native holy-days, the administration of heathen and Muhammadan laws, religious processions, and on other matters in respect to which Edwardes thought we acted in violation of Christian principles, the despatch ended with the well-known passage:—

'Before concluding this letter I am to state that Sir J. Lawrence has been led, in common with others since the occurrence of the awful events of 1857, to ponder deeply on what may be the faults and shortcomings of the British as a Christian nation in India. In considering topics such as those treated of in this despatch he would solely endeavour to ascertain what is our Christian duty. Having ascertained that according to our erring lights and conscience, he would follow it out to the uttermost, undeterred by any consideration. If we address ourselves to this task, it may, with the blessing of Providence, not prove too difficult for us. Measures have indeed been proposed as essential to be adopted by a Christian Government which would be truly difficult or impossible of execution. But on closer consideration it will be found that such measures are not enjoined by Christianity, but are contrary to its spirit. Sir John Lawrence does, I am to state, entertain the earnest belief that all those measures which are really and truly Christian can be carried out in India, not only without danger to British rule, but, on the contrary, with every advantage to its stability. Christian things done in a Christian way will never, the Chief Commissioner is convinced, alienate the heathen. About such things there are qualities which do not provoke nor excite distrust, nor harden to resistance. It is when unchristian things are done in the name of Christianity, or when Christian things are done in an unchristian way, that mischief and danger are occasioned. The difficulty is, amid the political complications, the conflicting social considerations, the fears and hopes of self-interest which are so apt to mislead human judgment, to discern clearly what is imposed upon us by Christian duty and what is not. Having discerned this, we have but to put it into practice. Sir John Lawrence is satisfied that within the territories committed to his charge he can carry out all those measures which are really matters of Christian duty on the part of the Government. And, further, he believes that such measures will arouse no danger; will conciliate instead of provoking; and will subserve the ultimate diffusion of the truth among the people.

'Finally, the Chief Commissioner would recommend that such measures and policy, having been deliberately determined on by the Supreme Government, be openly avowed and universally acted upon throughout the Empire; so that there may be no diversities of practice, no isolated, tentative, or conflicting efforts, which are, indeed, the surest means of exciting distrust; so that the people may see that we have no sudden or sinister designs; and so that we may exhibit that harmony and uniformity of conduct which befits a Christian nation striving to do its duty.'

Under the Lawrences, the connection between the Government and Christian missions had always been as close as official duty permitted. The policy pursued was that of the Charter of 1698 returned to in the Charter Act of 1813—the policy that prevailed in the days of Schwartz, when the East India Company was glad even to employ missionaries on diplomatic duties, and had not yet come to look upon the spread of Christian truth as dangerous to its interests. The events of the Mutiny deepened Lawrence's views on this subject, and elicited valuable opinions from many eminent men on the safety and advantage of a Christian policy. Lord Palmerston declared that it was our interest as well as our duty to promote the diffusion of Christianity as far as possible through the length and breadth of India; and Sir Charles Wood saw in every additional Christian an additional bond of union with England and an additional source of strength to the Empire. With a similar conviction, Lawrence advocated the raising of Native Christian regiments. He knew of no element of security except that of Christianity which could render it safe to increase tho proportion of Native troops, even when duly counterpoised as to caste and race. He expressed a strong conviction of the duty and wisdom of bringing into the service as many Christian Natives as possible. With such a force at command, he considered British rule would strike a new root in India. It was ignorance of the true nature of Christianity that made panic spread through our Indian army. The Sepoys imagined the Christian religion to consist in ceremonial arrangements like their own.

Valuing as he did 'the liberty to know, to utter, and to argue freely according to conscience, above all liberties,' Lawrence not only claimed it for himself, but opposed 'quiet persecution' as he called it, and the application of secular motives in any form to the spread of Christianity. While he believed that Christianity goes hand in hand with all the objects for which British rule exists in India, he had a profound conviction that it could only be extended by moral influences, voluntarily accepted. He conceded to the Native religions the same freedom he claimed for his own, being confident that the truth will in the end prevail. In this spirit he resisted the clamour which was raised for the destruction of religious buildings at Delhi, and in due time restored the Great Mosque to the Muhammadans. Afterwards, when he was

Governor-General, he gave back to them the Pearl Mosque at Agra, and, on the petition of the Muhammadans of Lahore, he restored to them the Grand Mosque in that city which had been desecrated by the Sikhs and long disused. This Mosque was the first in the Punjab in which prayers were offered for the Queen. There, every Friday, a blessing is now invoked on Her Majesty's reign.

The same spirit of toleration animated all Sir John Lawrence's proceedings. In Central India there is a petty State, Rájgarh, one of the many which were rescued from destruction by the establishment of the British Protectorate in Málwá. The Ruling Chief, who was a Rájput, had long shown a tendency towards Muhammadanism, and got thereby into difficulties with the brethren of his caste. Matters came to a head when Sir John Lawrence was Viceroy. It was reported that the Chief had undergone circumcision, and the feeling against him on this account, among his relatives and nobles, was so strong, that he proposed to abdicate and retire into private life. Inquiry, however, showed there was no charge of misgovernment against him, and that, except on the ground of change of creed, his people were satisfied with his rule. He was therefore maintained in power, and his people were informed that, so long as the government of the Chief was just, they must be loyal and obedient without reference to his creed. A year or two later, the Chief and his sons openly renounced the Hindu religion and embraced Muhammadanism.

taking a Muhammadan name which the British Government recognised, and receiving a Muhammadan title.

This case is a leading one, and has established in regard to the government of Native States the principle, which has long been accepted by the Legislature in civil affairs, that no rights shall be forfeited or impaired merely by change of religion or loss of caste. A Christian Government in a heathen or Muhammadan country could not, it might be thought, acknowledge any other principle. But the constitution of a Rájput State is so intimately interwoven with religious and caste observances, that the conversion of the Chief to another religion, which throws him outside the tribe or family, may involve serious constitutional changes; and only a few years before, when the leaning of the Rájgarh Chief to Muhammadanism began and his first troubles were adjusted, he had been told that a recurrence of the difficulties might make it necessary for him to abdicate and live in exile. The principle is now, however, clearly established. As a matter of fact, the Native States of India, other than the Rájputs, are mushroom growths, having a shorter history than our own. In some, like Bhopál, Haidarábád, Tonk, and others, the rulers are Muhammadan and the people are Hindu. In Kashmír we have a Muhammadan population under a Hindu ruler. What the British Government, as the imperial power, concerns itself with, is not the religious belief, in which rulers and people are alike left free to follow their convictions, but the good government of the country.

Before he left Lahore, Sir John Lawrence had been offered by Lord Stanley a seat in the Council of India which was formed when the Government was transferred to the Crown. He took his place on April 11th, 1859, soon after his arrival in London. His name was now familiar in the mouth of every one. The freedom of the cities of London and Glasgow was conferred formally upon him. He was saluted as the 'Organiser of Victory,' and the 'Saviour of India.' At a public assembly presided over by the Archbishop of Canterbury, an address was presented to him, signed by over 8,000 persons of all ranks in society. Oxford and Cambridge inscribed his name as a Doctor of Civil Law on their honorary rolls. Court favour was directed to him. He was fêted and made a guest in the houses of the great. But through it all he bore himself with the modesty and simplicity which had always distinguished him, and claimed a share in the honours for those who had shared with him the perils of the struggle, and by whose aid he acknowledged that his efforts to maintain the supremacy of England were crowned with success. He found his enjoyment in the bosom of his family, in the society of his friends, and in the quiet of his country home.

The work at the India Office was not congenial to him. He was out of place on a Board which had no administrative power, and where he found his cherished views on vital questions, such as that of a local army for India, overruled by a system of voting in which knowledge and experience of India counted only for one. After four and a half years of this work, he was nominated to be Viceroy and Governor-General of India in succession to Lord Elgin, under circumstances which I have already narrated. 'On the morning of November 30th, 1863,' says his biographer, 'Sir Charles Wood looked into Sir John Lawrence's room at the India Office with the pregnant announcement, "You are to go to India as Governor-General. Wait here till I return from Windsor with the Queen's approval." It was not till long after office hours that Sir Charles returned with the warm approval which he had sought and had obtained; and now the "imperial appointment, which is the greatest honour England has to give, except the government of herself," belonged to John Lawrence.' 'The Governor-Generalship is too good a post for a fellow like me,' he had said, when Sir Colin Campbell expressed a hope he might succeed Lord Canning. Now there was only one voice. The choice was as popular in England as in India. Men of every grade in society and every shade of political opinion agreed that the right man had been selected. Leaving his family behind him, he started from London on December 9th; landed in Calcutta on January 12th, 1864; and at once entered on his exalted office under the usual formalities.

CHAPTER VIII

FRONTIER AND FEUDATORY AFFAIRS

I HAVE said that Sir John Lawrence's Viceroyalty was an uneventful time. Great natural calamities by famine and cyclone fell upon the country, which called forth the philanthropic energies of Government and people. Commerce passed through an unexampled crisis, taxing skill and foresight. But the political atmosphere was calm. With the exception of little frontier wars, wasteful of resources that were sorely needed, there was nothing to divert the Government from the prosecution of schemes for the improvement of the physical and moral condition of the people.

On the North the land frontier of India extends along the range of the Himálaya mountains about 1,900 miles, across more than twenty-seven degrees of longitude. It marches with the independent countries of Bhután, Nepál, and Afghánistán, the petty State of Sikkim, the great feudatory State of Kashmír, and a multitude of small Rájput principalities round Simla and Kángra, survivals of the Hindu period prior to the successive waves of Muhammadan invasion. On the East the land boundary has since Lawrence's viceroyalty been greatly extended, and received a new political significance by the conquest of Upper Burma. On the North-west also the frontier has been pushed outward as the result of the Afghán war; but in 1864 it ran for over 800 miles from the snow peaks which close the Kágán valley, along the skirt of the Suláimán range to the province of Sind, and then by the Khelát State and adjacent territories to the sea. Down nearly to the Sind border, the mountain tribes flanking our territory are independent, warlike, revengeful, fanatical Patháns, who, with exception of the Mohmands, call no man master, not even the Amír of Kábul. Below them come the equally brave but less bigoted Biluch tribes, who pay a more or less fluctuating allegiance to the ruler of Khelát. It will be no matter of surprise that causes of unrest are always at work, and military operations are ever impending, on so extended a frontier, having political relations of so multiform a character with rulers who have to be managed by persuasion and diplomacy, with fierce clans full of religious fanaticism, with marauding tribes that know no law but the sword, and with naked head-hunting savages.

It was, as I have said, a dangerous war on the North-west frontier that finally settled the appointment of Sir John Lawrence to be Governor-General. On his way out, as he touched at Galle, he received a memorandum, written by Sir Bartle Frere, then Governor of Bombay, intended for the unknown successor to Lord Elgin, and containing a severe attack on the frontier policy pursued in the Punjab as compared with that which prevailed in Sind. 'I do not know,' wrote Sir John Lawrence, 'from whom Frere takes his information. I know he has no personal knowledge of the country himself. His own knowledge is limited to that of the Sind frontier, which in many essentials is different to that of the Punjab. From the borders of Sind northwards, the character of the people, both in the hills and on the plains, differs as you go along.' On such a frontier it is folly to apply a Procrustean policy. Nothing for instance could well be more different than the constitution of the Biluch tribes under their hereditary Chiefs and that of the Patháns with their tribal councils in which every man is equal, and with their clans and sections of clans which are ever at feud. In the one case, if you secure the Chieftain you secure the tribe; in the other you can succeed only by influencing general sentiment, which is to be reached by palaver and discussion or by bribery and self-interest. And the country is as different as the constitution of the tribes and the character of the people. On the Sind frontier the marauding mountaineers are separated from the alluvial plains of the Indus by twenty miles of desert open to the operations of cavalry and troops. Along the Suláimán range, where dwell the Patháns, the spurs run down into the cultivated valleys, the villages are pushed up on the slopes of the hills, and the surrounding country is broken up by deep ravines which render the attacks of robbers easy and their pursuit difficult. If therefore there was difference in the plan of treatment in the two provinces, it arose from difference of circumstances.

The policy adopted on the Punjab frontier was one of conciliation and defence:—

> By slow prudence to make mild
> A rugged people, and through soft degrees
> Subdue them to the useful and the good.

Neighbourly good offices were sedulously cultivated, and, while the clans were made to understand that there was no desire to interfere in their territories, they were taught that no aggression would be permitted on our own. The marches were held by a double line, the outer by Tribal Militia and the inner by the Frontier Force, both spread over a series of fortified posts. These were to give account of armed marauders. Friendly tribes were encouraged to trade. Fairs were established for their convenience. Deputations from them were received and hospitably entertained. Their sick were freely treated in our hospitals, and their boys were taught in our schools. Their tribesmen were taken into service, and even settled on lands within the British frontier on easy terms. Offences were punished by fine and the demand of compensation; if that proved unavailing, the recalcitrant tribe was excluded from our territories; and as a last resource a force of troops might be sent to bring them to reason. There can be no question that year by year this watchful and firm, though peaceful and conciliatory, policy has produced a marked change in the conduct of the Patháns tribes and a great improvement in our relations with them. But to extirpate border crime is beyond human power. Frontier raids, as Lord Dalhousie observed, are no more to be regarded as interruptions of the general peace in India, than the street brawls which appear among the every-day proceedings of a police court in London are regarded as indications of the existence of civil war in England. Punitive expeditions are a necessity of the situation. They will not cease till the other side of the line is held by civilised governments.

Between 1864 and 1869 there were several forays at various points, but only two were collisions which really disturbed the peace. One was a petty affair with the Bezotis of the Kohát Pass, the other a more serious encounter with the Patháns of the Black Mountain. The latter was caused by an attack of the tribes in July 1868, at the instigation of the Chief of Agror, upon a police post, the establishment of which he resented. Disturbances, in the course of which more than twenty British villages were destroyed, lasted till October, when troops were sent to punish the aggressors. A force of 12,000 men was employed, which penetrated without serious opposition to the crest of the Black Mountain, explored the enemy's country, occupied their strongholds, and reduced the tribes to submission for the time.

But a little cloud, very black while it lasted, arose on the opposite corner of the frontier soon after Sir John Lawrence landed in India. Our relations with

Bhután had never been intimate or even very friendly. They began in 1772, when Warren Hastings had to expel the Bhutánese from our border. Bhután was a dependency of Tibot, and at the intercession of the Teshu Lama a treaty of peace was concluded in 1774. The opportunity seemed favourable for establishing a friendly understanding, and George Bogle was despatched by Warren Hastings to Lassa to try to open up commercial intercourse. He would probably have succeeded but for the untimely death of the Teshu Lama. Turner's mission followed in 1783, but failed to break through Tibetan exclusiveness. For a long time thereafter no further attempt was made to penetrate into the countries on the northern frontier of Bengal. Our acquisition of Assam, in 1826, brought us into closer contact, chiefly in the way of depredations on villages in the plains, which the mountaineers looked upon as a happy hunting-ground. One more attempt was made—by Pemberton's mission in 1838—but the Bhután Government rejected the treaty that was proposed. Frontier affairs continued on a very bad footing. We tried to improve them by taking the management of Districts at the base of the hills and paying to Bhután the surplus revenues. But little good resulted. Bhután seemed to be in a chronic state of revolution and civil war, with no settled government. Outrages and aggressions led to remonstrances, reprisals, and threats of severer measures. Matters went from bad to worse, and war was on the point of breaking out, when the Mutiny of the Sepoy army called the British Government to a struggle for its own existence.

At last, in 1862, on the representations of the Bengal Government, Lord Canning agreed once more to try the expedient of a mission to explain our demands. This course was concurred in by Lord Elgin when he assumed the government. Owing, however, to the evasions and delays of the Bhutánese, and the reluctance of the Governor-General to force their hand, the mission did not start till the interregnum between the death of Lord Elgin and the arrival of Sir John Lawrence. The truth is the country was once more in the throes of revolution; the Spiritual and Temporal Kings of Bhután were puppets in the hands of a successful insurgent, the Tongso Penlo: there was no government with which permanent relations could be established. The mission left Dárjíling on December 4th, 1863, and returned on April 12th, 1864, having been not only received without honour but subjected to insult and outrage. With difficulty the Envoy got away from the capital under cover of night, after he had been compelled by threats of personal violence to sign a humiliating treaty, which the Government of India could only instantly repudiate. War was the inevitable consequence. After some military operations, the Bhutánese sued for peace, gave up the treaty extorted from the Envoy, and ceded the country lying at the foot of the hills, known as the Eighteen Dwárs, or Passes, receiving from us an annual payment of £5000 on condition of their future friendly conduct. The treaty added to the Queen's dominions a strip of territory about 180 miles long and from twenty to thirty miles broad.

Much hostile criticism was expended on the treaty at the time. European opinion in India is aggressive, and military opinion is dominant. Military men, smarting under a temporary check in which we had lost two guns, condemned Lawrence for granting the Bhutánese terms which were thought too easy. But the guns were restored as a preliminary condition of peace; and Lawrence, 'rich in saving common sense,' fought for peace, not for prestige. Nothing was to be gained by the prosecution of a war with the Bhutánese at any time, least of all when India was overwhelmed in commercial and financial troubles. The best proof that the terms were just lies in the fact that our relations with Bhután have ever since been better than they were before. During the recent difficulties with Tibet, the Bhután Government resisted the pressure put upon them to adopt an unfriendly attitude towards us.

Frontier affairs belong to the department of work which the Viceroy keeps in his own hands. So do the affairs of the dependent States of India. Of these there is a vast number—more than six hundred. They cover more than one-third of the Continent of India[1],

1	*Square miles.*	*Population in round numbers.*
All India	1,583,276	287,850,000
Native States ...	638,672	66,000,000

and contain more than one-fifth of the population. Their revenues are estimated to be £19,500,000, and they pay to the British Government an annual tribute of £750,000. These States differ greatly in size and importance. Hyderábád, for example, has an area of 82,000 square miles, a population of ten and a half millions, and a revenue of more than £3,000,000. At the other extreme there are States so small as to consist of only one or two villages with less than five hundred inhabitants and revenues which do not amount to £100 a year! Whatever be their political importance or insignificance, however, they have all some common features—they are not subject to British laws; they are subordinate to the British Government and under its protection and control; they are not permitted to combine or to enter into negotiations with each other or with any foreign power; their relations are with the British Government alone.

Our relations with them, it will easily be understood, are of the most varied kind. Some, like the great principalities of Rájputána, have survived shock after shock of foreign invasion, and exist from an age which procures for them religious veneration. Others represent the powerful lieutenants of the Great Mughal, who bit by bit assumed independence as the grip of the central power relaxed. Some were upheavals in the expiring convulsions of the Muhammadan Empire, which the *Pax Britannica* stereotyped. Some are the work of the British Government itself, created from territories it had conquered. The treaties and engagements with these States are legion. But of still greater importance, if possible, are the relations established by a long course of usage which exhibit the acknowledged and accepted conditions of British supremacy. The sovereign powers of all are limited in a greater or less degree. Some few possess the more distinctive attributes of a separate government; in others the powers of the Chiefs have been so reduced that the sovereignty almost disappears. In every case the residuary sovereignty vests in the British Crown.

In our relations with these States the Mutiny comes as a great line of cleavage. The decade preceding the revolt of the army had seen the British dominions largely extended by the absorption of Native States. Oudh had been annexed because of the King's misrule. One after another the States of Sátára, Jhánsi, and Nágpur had been treated as escheats. The Rájput principality of Karauli had been spared, but opinions had been expressed by Lord Dalhousie in the discussion of the case which, if acted on, would have undermined the oldest States in Rájputána. One small Rájput State, indeed—Baghát, in the Simla Hills—was actually treated as a lapse. It is true that neither the doctrine of escheat nor the practice was new. But they had never before been so logically or systematically enforced. The views of the Governor-General were well known. He believed that petty principalities, intervening within the British boundaries, might be made the means of annoyance to us, but could never be a source of strength. He expressed the opinion that advantage should be taken of every just opportunity to get rid of them by annexing them when there were no direct heirs. He had applied his principles to one of the largest States, and had argued for them in the case of one of the oldest. No Ruling Chief felt secure for the future, and there arose a general fear. All this was completely reversed by the Mutiny. The Native States rendered priceless service in the day of our distress. Lord Dalhousie's dictum that they could never be a source of strength was falsified. Speaking in the fulness of his gratitude, Lord Canning described them as 'breakwaters to the storm, which would otherwise have swept over us in one great wave.' 'The safety of our rule is increased,' he wrote, 'not diminished, by the maintenance of Native Chiefs well affected to us. . . . And should the day come when India shall be threatened by an external enemy, or when the interests of England elsewhere may require that her Eastern Empire shall incur more than ordinary risk, one of our best mainstays will be found in these Native States.'

Lord Canning restored the State of Baghát; and his parting gifts to the Chiefs of India were deeds, dated the day before he laid down the reins of office, in which he assured them, one by one, that the Queen desired to perpetuate their Princely Houses, that the policy of escheat was at an end, and that adopted heirs would be recognised. This announcement had already been made during Lord Canning's celebrated progress through the provinces of Upper India. It was received with universal joy. At Gwalior the good news was welcomed 'with rejoicing very like that which would have marked the birth of an heir.' The present writer was an eye-witness of the satisfaction with which the announcement was hailed. He remembers the long-drawn sigh of relief which escaped from the assembled Chiefs when the new policy was first made known at the Cawnpur Darbár, on November 4th, 1859. He remembers the interview at which one of the most powerful Chiefs in Central India told Lord Canning that, though his family had ruled for eleven hundred years, the assurance given 'had dispelled an evil wind that had long been blowing upon him.' A new era was at once introduced. The Doctrine of Lapse became a dead doctrine—buried and put away. Confidence took the place of general mistrust. The British Government stood out as the paramount power in India more clearly than it had ever done before. 'There is a reality in the suzerainty of the sovereign of England,' wrote Lord Canning, 'which has never existed before, and which is not only felt, but eagerly acknowledged, by the Chiefs.' Henceforth the Native States became part and parcel of the British Empire, with whose prosperity their interests were identified, and the Queen became in fact the Empress of India.

Sir John Lawrence's relation to this new policy was twofold. It was from his province of the Punjab that the proposal emanated to recognise adopted heirs; and it fell to him, almost in immediate succession to Lord Canning, to give the first direction to the principles which followed from the change, and which have since gradually developed into an established system of political law.

In his early public life Lawrence was an annexationist. He drank at the same fountain as Lord Dalhousie and imbibed the principles of his great master and friend. As Magistrate of Delhi he had seen the worst side of a licentious Court, and the rampant evils caused by a multitude of petty Native Chiefships which the British Government preserved from extinction, but abstained from guiding or controlling. He had seen with satisfaction the little Chiefs of the Cis-Sutlej States reduced to the position of ordinary subjects. He had refused to re-establish the principalities in Kángra, which the Sikhs had destroyed. He had advocated the annexation of the Punjab, and one of his first acts as Chief Commissioner had been to deprive the Nawáb of Mamdot of sovereign power, which he had abused, and to bring his territory under British jurisdiction. He had seen without a pang of regret the Kingdom of Oudh absorbed within the red line. 'Anything short of it,' he wrote, 'is a mistake. Will not all the people rejoice, except the fiddlers, barbers, and that genus? I wish I was thirty-five instead of forty-five, and had to put it in order.'

But the Mutiny revealed to him, as it did to

Canning, the value of our Native allies, without whose co-operation it is not too much to say that Delhi could not have been recovered. Lawrence pressed for an ample and generous reward to the Chiefs who had stood by us, and he procured for them large additions to their territories. But there was one reward dearer to their heart than all. What advantage was an accession of territory if, after all, their States should lapse in default of heirs? So the three Phúlkían Chiefs[1], in February 1858, put forth requests for the recognition of adopted heirs. Sir John Lawrence supported the prayer; but it was refused by the Government of India. Under the influence and advice of Lawrence, however, who was now in the Secretary of State's Council, the Government in England decided that the boon should be granted to them as a special case. But long before Lord Canning received these orders, he had discovered for himself that in the concession of the privilege of adoption lay the solution of many political difficulties; and he had already announced his change of policy. He conferred the right upon the Phúlkían Chiefs in open Darbár, at Ambála, on January 20th, 1860. On this question Lawrence was prepared to go even further than Lord Canning. One of his last acts as Viceroy was to assure the Mahárájá of Kashmír that, should heirs of his body fail him and no formal adoption

[1] The three Chiefs—Patiála, Jínd, and Nábha—are so called because of their descent from a common ancestor named Chaudri Phúl.

have been made, his wishes in regard to the succession of a collateral relation would be respected.

Loyalty to the Crown and fidelity to engagements were the conditions on which Canning guaranteed the perpetuity of the Native States. Good government was the condition on which Lawrence maintained the ruling Chiefs in power. Kingdoms were no longer annexed for misgovernment; but Chiefs were deposed or visited with marks of displeasure. Jhábua was fined and deprived of honours for a serious abuse of power. Tonk was deposed and sent into exile. On Chiefs who were given to evil ways Lawrence would bring all his personal influence to bear by kindly advice or solemn warning. 'A Chief who ranks so high,' he said to one, 'should also take among men a similar position for justice, for benevolence, and for the excellence with which his affairs are managed. It is my earnest desire that this should be the ambition of Your Highness.' But it was from the education of the young Chiefs that he hoped for real improvement. Every now and then long minorities occur when the Native States are necessarily brought under close supervision. Sir John Lawrence made use of all such opportunities by requiring the regents to associate the young Chief with them in the discussion of important matters and to train him to the business of the State. He earnestly pressed Native rulers to have their sons carefully trained. 'I urge you to instruct your sons, and even your daughters,' he said to the Chiefs at Lahore, as he addressed them in their own language, which they were unaccustomed to hear from Viceregal lips. And to the great Chiefs of Rájputána and Central India, assembled at Agra, he said, 'The art of governing wisely and well is a difficult one, which is only to be attained by much thought and care and labour. . . . Of all fame that great men can acquire, that alone is worth having which is accorded to a just and beneficent ruler. The names of conquerors and heroes are forgotten. But those of virtuous and wise Chiefs live for ever.'

In all this there was nothing exactly new in principle. It had long been admitted as a consequence of our supremacy that we are bound in duty to interfere in Native States to prevent gross oppression or injustice. The limits and conditions of that interference had never been defined, but it was felt in a general way that misgovernment in a Native State upheld by British power was misgovernment for which the British Government was to some extent responsible. Space forbids more than a mere enumeration of some of the seeds of political law that were sown in Lawrence's time. I have already noted the principle of religious liberty established in the Rájgarh case. *Satí* received its deathblow in Kotah. The practice of burying lepers alive was stamped out in Sirohi and Márwár. Female infanticide was put down among the Purihar Rájputs of Jigni. The last remnants of slavery were eradicated in Kuch Behar. Capital punishment for cow-killing was forbidden. The British civil and criminal jurisdiction was secured on all main lines of railway running through Native States.

The key to the understanding of our feudatory relations is the principle, so luminously expounded by Sir Henry Maine[1], that the attributes of sovereignty over Native States are divided between the Chiefs and the Crown in degrees which vary with each State; and that the subjects of the Chiefs are subjects also of the Queen to the extent to which she shares the sovereignty. This principle was clearly formulated with reference to the Rájás of Káthiáwár and the Chiefs of the Central Provinces. On the same principle the liability of the subjects of Feudatory States to British consular jurisdiction abroad was asserted, and the same consular protection was claimed for them as for British subjects, inasmuch as they are the subjects of powers that have no foreign relations, but are, in international concerns, represented by the British Government and form in fact part of the British Empire.

Since that time Indian political law has been largely developed by treaty, by sufferance, by growing usage, and by the reasonable construction of *de facto* relations in actual cases which have from time to time arisen. Vast improvement also has been made in the administration of Native States, under the guidance and control of the British Government. Those are for the most part the best governed that have imitated British methods without slavishly adopting British

[1] Minutes dated March 22nd and May 11th, 1864.

institutions. Personal rule is growing weaker, and giving place to government by law. Codes of law have been adopted, regular courts of justice have been established, fixed assessments of the public burdens have been introduced, schools and hospitals have been opened, railways and canals have been constructed, and, in short, the usual machinery of regular government has been set at work. And though now and again we may be startled by scandalous cases of oppression and injustice, it is no longer possible for any Native ruler to commit himself to a course of crime, tyranny, and general misgovernment as in the days of old.

CHAPTER IX

AGRARIAN AFFAIRS

ALTHOUGH Lawrence was fully alive to the political advantage of maintaining Native States, and gratefully recognised all they had done for us, he always adhered to the opinion he formed when he was a District Officer as to the blessings conferred by British rule on the people of India. He freely admitted that it would be unreasonable to expect strong attachment to a Government so alien as ours, from a people to whom the miseries from which the country was delivered had become matter of ancient history. But he held it to be unquestionable that the masses of the population are more prosperous, and ought, if they knew their own interests, to be happier in British territory than under Native rule.

Other views had been expressed in the House of Commons by high authority in the debate on the restoration of Mysore to a Native ruler, and Sir John Lawrence took the opportunity to have the question discussed. The correspondence is interesting in so far as it brings out points in which our Government offends against the usages, or prejudices, or legitimate wishes of the people. It may be useful in so far as it suggests measures, not inconsistent with our general principles of administration, for making English rule more popular. But in the main the discussion was academic. For it is not to be seriously disputed that in everything which affects the maintenance of peace, the security of life and property, the administration of humane laws, the fixing and equalising of taxation, the prevention of disease, the relief of suffering, religious and political freedom, education, the extension of cultivation, the development of the country by roads and railways and canals, the promotion of commerce—everything, in short, that contributes to the security, the comfort, and the convenience of life—the British Government has conferred blessings on the people of India such as never entered into the mind of Hindu Kings or Muhammadan Emperors in the most palmy days of their power. Unless, indeed, we honestly believe this, we have no vocation in India and had better retire to our ships.

What the masses of India above all things desire is—to be let alone. So long as they are treated with justice and sympathy they care not by whom they are governed. As a matter of fact, the Mughals were as foreign in race, in religion, and in manners as ourselves. But it is the misfortune of the mission of England that it cannot leave the people of India alone. 'In doing the best we can for the people,' said Sir John Lawrence, 'we are bound by our conscience, and not by theirs.' 'We aim at being just and strong,' as Edwardes wrote, 'and is there any such frightful bore in the whole world as your Aristides?' To be popular is not always within the reach of those who deserve it. But it *is* possible to ensure a general contentment; and to make the people content, so far as he could do so without sacrificing the higher ends of English rule, was the aim which Lawrence put before himself in all his measures.

A prosperous and contented peasantry he considered to be a more solid foundation of our power than a landed aristocracy. This principle underlay all the differences with his brother Henry in the early Punjab days. Large grants of land or money to the Native gentry seemed to him to be so much taken from the people, with no corresponding advantage to the Government. 'I cannot see the political value,' he said, 'of such allies as Tej Singh, Dína Náth, and others; but it seems to me that we have been even munificent to them. I do not think that in the event of a disturbance any of them would act against us, or, indeed, would have any inducement to do so; and moreover, if they did, they would do us no harm.' Perhaps the clash of dispute with his brother led to expression of extreme views. For his biographer notes that, when Sir John became Chief Commissioner and had the undivided responsibility on his shoulders, his policy began so to gravitate towards that of Henry as to draw down a rebuke from Lord Dalhousie, 'who appealed from the John Lawrence of the present to the John Lawrence of former days.' This question, like so many others, was reduced to its true proportions by the Mutiny. In the Punjab the great nobles have assumed the position of Honorary Magistrates and Revenue Officers; and recently, on the recommendation of the present writer, a concession has been made, similar to that granted to Ruling Chiefs, which admits of the transmission of their privileges to adopted heirs, in the case of those who distinguish themselves by loyalty and good service.

But the question of a landed aristocracy in the Punjab was of little importance compared with that of tenant-right, with which Sir John Lawrence had to deal. The Punjab is a country of peasant-proprietors, not of feudal barons. Out of about twenty-five millions of acres of land, about three millions are tilled by occupancy-tenants, six millions by tenants-at-will, and all the rest by the proprietary communities. In the Sikh times property in the land was never regarded. The matter was one of revenue. Proprietors were ousted by the Government and new men put in according as they could or could not pay the land-tax. Land was of no value. Often it was a burden, involving responsibilities to the State with no corresponding protection. Competition was not for lands to cultivate, but for tenants to cultivate them. Hence it came to pass that difficulties between landlord and tenant never arose; many landlords were glad to get their fields cultivated for no rent at all so long as the revenue was paid; as a matter of fact, tenants were seldom evicted by the landlord; and when the Punjab was annexed the tenants were found to have held for generations a strong position hardly inferior to that of the proprietors. Those who had cultivated their holdings for twelve years before annexation were therefore recorded as occupancy-tenants. Landowners raised no objections; they rather welcomed the arrangement.

Fifteen years later the revenue-settlements fell in, and had to be revised and renewed. Meanwhile the limitation of the land-tax, and the peace and security established by British rule, had given an enormous value to what was before worthless. Landowners became eager to claim rights which once they had been careless about. At the same time, some of the Officers entrusted with the revision of the revenue-settlement had imbibed extreme views of ownership and were disinclined to recognise a double right in the soil. In endeavouring to remedy mistakes which may have been made, they fell into an opposite error and disturbed beneficial interests which had been enjoyed for more than a quarter of a century. In one division of the province, out of 46,000 heads of agricultural households who had been recorded as occupancy-tenants, more than three-fourths were, by a stroke of the pen, reduced to the position of tenants-at-will, liable to eviction and rack-rent. This was really an agrarian revolution, destroying interests in land which, as Sir Henry Maine observed, had been 'enjoyed by thousands of persons for a period very little, if at all, short of the time which in England would ripen those interests into vested rights, even though acquired originally by naked wrong.' Sir Donald Macleod, who was then Lieutenant-Governor, declared the state of things thus brought about to be 'rapidly undermining all good feeling between the most important classes of the agricultural population.'

The attitude which Sir John Lawrence took up was very simple and very just. The property in dispute was entirely the creation of the British Government. The Government had sacrificed revenue in reducing the assessment of the land: it had thus created a rent where none previously existed. The Government maintained law and order: it had thus given a great value to what before was valueless. The proper way to settle the difficulty was to deal with each interest in a fair and liberal spirit, and so to apportion the property we had created as to give to the proprietor a large share and at the same time leave to the cultivator a sufficient reward for his labour. Thanks to his love of justice and strong practical common sense, the Punjab Tenancy Act, which was framed by his Government, solved the question with singular fairness, defining the circumstances under which occupancy rights were to be recognised, and granting compensation for unexhausted improvements in cases of eviction. The immediate effect of the Act in five Districts of the Punjab was to restore 63,000 persons to the position of occupancy-tenants who had been summarily reduced to the position of tenants-at-will. Writing fourteen years afterwards, the Lieutenant-Governor (Sir Robert Egerton) said, 'Regarded by some at the time as a confiscation of proprietary right, it has been found defective only in the comprehensiveness of its provisions for maintaining the status of the tenants, while in the greater part of the province it is the bulwark and charter of a contented peasantry.'

In Oudh there was a violent storm over the same question of tenant-right under circumstances almost the reverse of those in the Punjab. No measures undertaken by Sir John Lawrence called forth so much ignorant and hostile criticism as the protection he gave to subordinate land-tenures in Oudh. Some said he was trying to upset the policy by which Lord Canning had pacified the country; others that he was deliberately sowing discord between landlord and tenant. He was accused of breaking faith with the great landowners and of bringing unfair pressure to bear upon the nobles of the province to make them give in to his views. The cry was taken up in England. The authority of the Secretary of State was invoked. But Lawrence faced the storm without flinching. 'One of the main causes of the excitement in this matter,' he wrote to his friend Captain Eastwick, 'is that several Englishmen have obtained estates in Oudh. The question also bears on the present struggle in Bengal; and so nearly all the Press, as representing the Native landholders on the one side and the English planter on the other, are arrayed against me. But this is no reason why I should not stand to my guns, and do what I believe to be fair and just!' And to Sir Charles Wood: 'What could make me take the course I have done in favour of the Ryots of Oudh but a strong sense of duty? . . . Of my own free will I will not move, knowing as I do that I am right in the course which has been adopted. Did ever any one hear of the Government of India learning that a class of men were not having fair play at the time of settlement, and then failing to interfere or to issue such orders as the case appeared to demand?'

What happened was briefly this: Oudh is a country, not of peasant proprietors like the Punjab, but of feudal barons, known by the name of Tálukdárs; they are two hundred and seventy-two in number, and at the time of the annexation of Oudh, in February 1856, they had possession of two-thirds of the province. Under the system of revenue-administration that was introduced the rights and position of these barons were ignored. No one now doubts that gross injustice was done to them. With few exceptions they went against us in the Mutiny, and the peasantry followed them *en masse*. In due time there came a great reactionary policy. The pendulum of prejudice swung as far in favour of the Tálukdárs as it had formerly swung against them. Lord Canning's famous Proclamation confiscating the proprietary-right in the soil of Oudh, which was issued on the fall of Lucknow, in March 1858, had three objects in view. It was not intended to be a permanent deprivation of rights, but to punish those who persisted in rebellion after life and honour had been guaranteed; to provide the means of rewarding those who should promptly submit; and to enable Government to attach such conditions to the grants as would remedy the injustice previously done and secure the fealty and good service of the grantees. And the Proclamation was so skilfully used by Sir Robert Montgomery, then Chief Commissioner of Oudh, that within a few months two-thirds of the rebel nobles had tendered their allegiance, and received back their estates. A permanent hereditary and transferable proprietary-right in their estates was thereupon conferred on them. 'This right is, however, conceded,' their title-deeds went on to say, 'subject to any measure which the Government may think proper to take for the purpose of protecting the inferior Zamíndárs and village occupants from extortion and of upholding their rights in the soil in subordination to the Tálukdárs.'

In carrying out this policy no enquiry into existing rights was made. The local authorities assumed that rights were to be recognised precisely as they stood at the date of annexation, and that subordinate proprietors who had previously lost their possessions could not recover them. They further assumed that all beneficial interests had been destroyed in the anarchy preceding annexation and that no distinction between privileged tenants and tenants-at-will was to be made.

This omission to enquire into facts appeared to Lawrence preeminently unjust. He held that every man was entitled to a fair hearing. He maintained that, while the nobility as a body were an ancient aristocracy, who had held their estates for many generations, others were creatures of a day, who had sprung up during the gross misrule preceding annexation. It was, therefore, only the barest justice to give a reasonable period of limitation for the recovery of rights lost in the time of anarchy. Fortunately, the Tálukdárs were a reasonable body of men. A compromise was soon effected, through the instrumentality of Sir John Strachey, the Chief Commissioner, the result of which was that sub-proprietors who had lost their rights within twelve years preceding annexation were reinstated, and persons who within thirty years had fallen from the position of proprietor to tenant obtained the position of tenant with right of occupancy, holding at privileged rents. By this means about one-fifth of the cultivators of the soil in Oudh received rights of occupancy in the lands they tilled.

So far from being an interference with Lord Canning's policy, this measure was the complement of it, giving effect to the condition which he had inserted in the deeds. It was effected with the full consent and approval of the nobles, and it adjusted the interests of three parties in the soil—the nobles, the under-proprietors, and the tenants. But for the courage of Lawrence and his love of justice, the under-proprietors would have been sacrificed and the whole body of the cultivators of Oudh would have been left to competition-rents, whereby agrarian troubles would have been sharply intensified. 'When the vast importance of the interests concerned is considered,' said Sir William Mansfield[1] (Lord Sandhurst), from his place in Council, when the Oudh Rent Bill was discussed, 'it was not too much to say that the passage of this law would be deemed hereafter a bright illustration of the history of the Viceregal reign, and that it would throw into the shade feats of government and policy which the public at present might consider more brilliant.'

I would gladly avoid the details of these questions. They are dry and repellent. But notice of them cannot be omitted if we would know the fundamental principles of Lawrence's administration. 'His ideal,' says Cust, 'which I have often heard from his lips, of a country thickly cultivated by a fat, contented yeomanry, each riding his own horse, sitting under his own fig-tree, and enjoying his rude family comforts, may not have been the ideal of a State in the nineteenth century politically free; but for a people whose destiny it has been for centuries to be conquered, domestic comforts and the enjoyment of their own customs, their own religion and their own language, soften the sting of foreign domination.' In such a prosperous peasantry too he saw the sustaining power of the country in seasons of drought and famine like that which has again and again fallen upon Districts of India. Lawrence's sympathies with

[1] Speech on Oudh Rent Bill, July 22nd, 1868.

this class were strong. He was the first to secure to tenants the right to improve their property by the reclamation of waste-lands, by drainage, and by the construction of works for the supply and storage of water and the like. In Oudh, the North-Western Provinces, and the Punjab, he removed some iniquitous laws which made the property of tenants who improved their holdings liable to confiscation at the will of the landlord, and he secured to evicted tenants fair compensation for unexhausted improvements.

It was always a matter of deep regret to Sir John Lawrence that tenants in Bengal had been left, for nearly three-quarters of a century, without the protection which Lord Cornwallis had promised them when the Permanent Settlement was introduced, in 1793. It is well known that in Bengal, as elsewhere in India, the cultivators had beneficial rights in the soil. These rights were no doubt indefinite, having been greatly encroached upon during the Muhammadan rule. But they were none the less real and dearly prized. Local enquiry at the time would have defined and adjusted them. But no enquiry was made. The Government contented itself with reserving, in the Proclamation of the Permanent Settlement, a general right of interference for the protection of subordinate tenures. Again and again this right to protection was affirmed. But until 1859 no Act was passed to give effect to it. The law remained entirely one-sided. As a consequence, the rights of the cultivators which were undefined and unrecorded went down before those which the law distinctly recognised. No doubt the disintegration of the rights of the children of the soil was a very gradual process. At first population was sparse; waste-land was abundant; and it was long before agrarian questions became acute. But if the mills ground slowly they ground exceeding small. New relations of custom and contract sprang up. Property changed hands. Tenures became subdivided and complicated. The people grew and multiplied and pressed more and more upon the land. Every year's delay increased the difficulty of the problem.

In 1859 an honest attempt was made to grapple with the question and to define the classes that needed protection and the nature of their rights. But the result was not fortunate. The Act which was passed gave to many cultivators a privileged status, but it gave no protection to customary rights, and overlooked many important local tenures. In fact it was passed without sufficient enquiry, and it introduced disturbances more often than it quieted them. When Sir John Lawrence became Viceroy the question was a burning one, exciting evil passions on both sides. 'These things,' he wrote, 'are never out of my mind, night or day; but how to reconcile people to what is wise and politic and good for both—there is the rub. I fear that the Ryots will never have fair play. There are too many and too strong interests against them. There will be much abuse heaped on our heads; but this we can bear.'

It was not a matter to be dealt with hurriedly. Full enquiry was what was needed; and Sir John Lawrence pressed the Lieutenant-Governor of Bengal to take the matter up and ascertain by careful investigation the real bearings of the question on all interests in the land. It did not fall to him to see the final issue in the Bengal Tenancy Act of 1885. Long years of patient enquiry were needed. But Lawrence set the stone rolling. It was he who originated the enquiries which had their consummation in this much-needed and long-deferred measure.

CHAPTER X

FAMINE—PUBLIC WORKS—FINANCE

IN the second year of his Viceroyalty the Lower Provinces of Bengal were overtaken by a calamity which in magnitude had not been seen for nearly a century. The rainfall of the year 1865 had been generally capricious, irregular, and scanty, and ceased altogether in the middle of September. Consequently there was a failure of the rice crop, which ripens in December. This is the most important crop of the year, furnishing the food of the people and regulating the prices of the market. Over many Districts scarcity extended, deepening in some into great suffering and mortality, and in Orissa into intense famine. Symptoms of the coming distress showed themselves at an early date. The excise revenue, which is said to be an index of the prosperity of the people, began to fall off largely.

Before September was out the price of rice in some parts of Orissa was at famine rates; and by the end of October the whole country was in panic. The markets were closed; the rice trade stopped; the landless and labouring classes were reduced to extreme destitution. From January onward the famine deepened in intensity. Prices went up and up, and by June the state of things was appalling. The ordinary price of the rice used for food is less than a farthing and a half per pound. Where it could be bought at all it went up to 2*d*., 2½*d*., 3½*d*. in the chief towns; and in the interior of Districts to 11*d*. a pound. For five months prices in the best-supplied markets ranged from five to ten times, and in the Districts at about thirty-five times, the ordinary rates! In many places rice could not be purchased at all, and money was useless. In the three Districts of Orissa the daily average number of persons receiving charitable relief from June to November was 52,686, two-thirds of whom received it gratuitously and the rest in return for light labour. Many died when they received the food, which their exhausted powers could not assimilate.

It was long hoped that the prices ranging in Orissa would attract supplies from outside and bring out the stocks that might be stored in the country. But there were no stocks in Bengal to meet a tithe of the demand, and nothing came in from outside markets. Hitherto Orissa had been a rice-exporting country. The rice stocks had been depleted by the export of nearly 55,000 tons in the two previous years. Orissa consists of two parts—ranges of hills running back into the plateau of the Central Provinces, and the alluvial country between these mountains and the sea. The hill tract is broken up into Tributary

States, under Native Chiefs; the plains are ordinary British territory, the creation of the 'land-making' rivers so graphically described in Hunter's *Orissa*. From the West by the rivers no aid was to be hoped for; they traversed a country where scarcity prevailed. Eastward the coast is inhospitable, exposed as the season advances to the full force of the monsoon. Native craft cannot live in such seas, and the coasting trade ceases in March. From North and South the traffic was carried by road over unbridged rivers, 'slowly and tediously, as ancient Officers may have travelled in the days of Asoka.' Scarcity reigned in the Districts round, and prices prevailed which made it unprofitable to penetrate through to Orissa. A bag or two came down the Mahánadí from Sambalpur. Otherwise not a sack of grain was attracted. In short, as the Famine Commissioners afterwards described the situation, 'the people, shut up in a narrow province between pathless jungles and an impracticable sea, were in the condition of passengers in a ship without provisions.'

Relief works were established at an early date, and Local Committees were formed for the distribution of charity. In January Sir John Lawrence made a grant of £50,000 for works; and afterwards of £60,000 more, the balance of a former famine fund, for charitable distribution. But the works very soon came to a standstill. Wages were paid in money and not in food; and money had no purchasing power, for rice could not be had. In the District of Purí which suffered most, only £2500 of the grant for works had been spent up to the end of May. Slowly the conviction forced itself on the authorities that not money was wanted, but food, which must be thrown into the country by the Government. The Government of India advanced to Bengal £200,000 for the purchase of rice, and promised unlimited funds. The import by steamship was vigorously taken up. But by this time the monsoon had burst on the coast. Landing the rice was a difficult and dangerous operation. The country boats often 'struggled for days against wind and current before reaching the landing-place, and not unfrequently went to the bottom.' In the open road-stead of Purí it took seven weeks to unload one steamer! Altogether it is estimated that, allowing for short weight and losses, only 8750 tons were imported up to the end of October. 'Every maund of rice landed from June to October saved a life [1], whether it was sold, given away, or stolen.' That is to say, some 245,000 souls were rescued from death.

As if to crush out of the wretched people the last pulse of hope, the rivers opened their sluices in September, overwhelming a thousand square miles of country, submerging the homesteads of a million and a quarter of people, and drowning the new crops to a depth of from three to fifteen feet for more than thirty days. Sir William Hunter has drawn a picture of the beneficent and malignant working of these rivers, in his chapter on The Calamities of Orissa, which no pencil

[1] *Famine Report*, par. 288.

can surpass. Drought may come once in a century or so, but devastation is every year impending from the rage of rivers, whose beds are hoisted by silt above the level of the country and whose channels afford an outlet for only half the volume of water they receive. From the calamities of 1866 it is estimated that one-fourth of the population of the alluvial Districts perished.

Such an awful calamity touched the heart of the English people; but it brought no help from England. Distress at home absorbed the public attention. The public of India, however, headed by the Viceroy, rose to the occasion. The Calcutta Committee disbursed £60,000 in relief. Sir John Lawrence was not backward. His recollection of the famines in his early service, when he was a District Officer, filled him with apprehension. He has been blamed for want of vigour in not pressing the Bengal Government to more active measures. Nothing could be more unjust. He sent the Lieutenant-Governor to Orissa to see things with his own eyes. Personally he was in favour of the importation of rice from the first, and urged it as early as November 1865. But his opinion was not shared by his Council[1] and was therefore not acted upon. The Lieutenant-Governor also states[2] that 'His Excellency the Viceroy consulted me personally as to the proposal to import rice into Bengal and Orissa,

[1] *Secretary of State's Despatch, Public,* No. 99, dated July 25, 1867, para. 7.

[2] *Blue Book,* May 31, 1867, p. 143, note.

both at the time at which it was made and afterwards when I returned from Cuttack in February. His Excellency was strongly inclined to act upon the proposal, but yielded to my opinion and that of others that it was not expedient or necessary.' Had Lawrence's proposals been adopted, many lives would have been saved.

The first lesson taught by the famine was the necessity of adopting effective measures for the irrigation of the province of Orissa, the control of its rivers, and the improvement of communications both by sea and land. But a powerful stimulus was also given to schemes of irrigation all over India for the increase of the food supply, and to railways and roads for its distribution. For twenty years Sir John Lawrence had been a constant and strenuous advocate of irrigation works. During his rule in the Punjab £880,000 had been spent on canals. He found the question of irrigation works before the Government when he came out as Viceroy. He took it up warmly at once and used all his influence, publicly and privately, to press its importance. Water in India, as Samuel Laing said, 'is more than gold; it is *life*.' Irrigation works had been starved. Progress had been delayed by two causes. Barracks for the European troops swallowed up available resources; and great works of irrigation could only be undertaken on well-considered plans which took much time to prepare.

Sir John Lawrence grappled with both difficulties.

He proposed, and the Secretary of State consented, that when the surplus revenues are insufficient to meet the requirements of the country in reproductive works, the money shall be raised by loan and the interest only charged to the expenditure of the year. He also created a Department of Irrigation, with Colonel Richard Strachey as its Superintendent, to mature plans and projects, and engaged a large staff of civil engineers from England to carry them out. Lawrence held that it was better for the people and the public interests that such works should be constructed by the State than by private companies. 'I am strongly for the first course,' he wrote, 'but I am content to accept the latter rather than have no canals.' When the Orissa irrigation project got into difficulties in the hands of a private company, he bought it up. New projects were prosecuted through State agency. In the last two years of his Viceroyalty £1,500,000 were borrowed for reproductive works, and about £1,250,000 of it were spent on great works of irrigation. Schemes were projected, under the advice of Colonel Richard Strachey, which were estimated to cost £30,000,000 within the next ten years.

All through his term of office Sir John Lawrence had to struggle with the weight of financial difficulties. He assumed the Viceroyalty in the middle of a money famine. Money was everywhere scarce and dear, and the country was passing through a great commercial crisis. The American War had thrown upon India the whole demand of Europe for cotton. Prices went up with startling rapidity. In 1860 the price of cotton was about £44 a ton; in 1863 it was double; in 1864 it stood at £189 a ton. In four years the price had more than quadrupled. Enormous fortunes were made and the peasantry in the cotton-growing Districts grew rich. At the large ports wages almost reached European rates. Bank interest at one time touched 15 per cent. Government securities fell. As there were few legitimate means for the investment of the accumulating wealth, speculation was stimulated in the wildest and most reckless way. 'Companies were started for every imaginable purpose—banks and financial associations, land reclamation, trading, cotton cleaning, pressing and spinning companies, coffee companies, shipping and steamer companies, hotel companies, livery stables and veterinary companies, and companies for making bricks and tiles. The shares of most of these companies were sold at high premia as soon as they were brought into the market[1].' Shares in the Back Bay Company in Bombay, on which only £500 had been paid up, fetched at public auction the enormous sum of £2,650!

The effect of this wild speculation was most felt in Bombay. But it extended to Calcutta, and in some degree all over India. Persons with small fixed incomes found it difficult to live; some were brought almost to starvation. The salaries of subordinate establishments had to be raised all over the country

[1] *Report of Commissioners on Failure of Bank of Bombay*, p. 2.

With the prospect of the close of the War came the inevitable reaction. Cotton went suddenly down for a time to about £56 a ton. Commercial houses and banks fell together like packs of cards. One Parsi firm failed for three millions sterling, another for two, and so on. The Bank of Bombay, which had committed itself to a reckless system of unsecured advances, went into voluntary liquidation notwithstanding the grant of Government support, having dissipated £1,890,000 out of a total capital of £2,090,000! Commercial confidence was gone. Shares were unsaleable. Government securities became as inflated as they had been depressed, and were for a time the principal means of mercantile remittances. The commercial cyclone however cleared the atmosphere, and things gradually recovered, going up in Bombay with a leap almost as suddenly as they went down, and then settling into steady and sound development. No ordinary statecraft was needed to steer the ship safely through the storm. If Sir John Lawrence had been furnished at the proper time with the information he called for as to the state of affairs in the Bank of Bombay, the severity of the collapse to the public might perhaps have been mitigated.

Added to all this commercial dislocation, there was a strong demand for improved administration. At best the Native Police and Judicial Services, the subordinates in the Customs, Post Office and other Departments, were much underpaid. Their salaries had to be increased; the pay of the Covenanted Civil

Service in the old Non-Regulation provinces had to be equalised with that elsewhere; the expenditure on Forests was more than doubled; the grant for Education was doubled; the cost of the Medical Services was nearly trebled by the increase of pay and the creation of a Department of Sanitation. The total expenditure went up during Lawrence's Viceroyalty from forty-five and three quarters to fifty-four and a half millions sterling. It was absolutely necessary also to house the European army properly. The lives of the men depended on it. The barrack accommodation, provided with the best scientific and sanitary appliances of the day for the health, comfort, and recreation of the men, was estimated to cost ten millions sterling to be spread over five years; and it was decided to pay the whole out of revenue. The expenditure began in 1864, and up to 1869 only $4\frac{3}{4}$ millions were spent, leaving $5\frac{1}{4}$ millions for future years. The army was reduced from 70,000 Europeans and 127,000 Natives in 1864 to 62,000 Europeans and 122,000 Natives in 1869. But nearly the whole saving was swallowed up in the increased cost of rationing the soldiers, and in measures for the promotion of the health and efficiency of the troops, so that the actual expenditure on the army in India stood at £12,990,000 at the close of Lawrence's term of office as compared with £13,182,000 when it began. Two little wars were also provided for out of revenue as well as a large share of the cost of famine relief, more than a million for transport vessels, and nearly half a million for the site of the India Office in London.

Need it be wondered at, that, with one exception, the years of Sir John Lawrence's Viceroyalty were years of deficit[1] to the amount of nearly $3\frac{3}{4}$ millions. Had the barracks been treated as Public Works Extraordinary and paid for by loan instead of from revenue, as some experts argued they should have been, and as is being done with barracks in England at the present day, there would have been a surplus of a million on the five years. As matters stood, there was a deficit of $3\frac{3}{4}$ millions, and the effect was that the barracks came to be paid to that extent from borrowed money and only one million from revenue. The clear financial principle however established in Lawrence's reign was the provision for reproductive works by loan, thereby affording the means so urgently needed for the development of the country and its protection against calamities of season. In the

[1] The actual figures are:—

Year.	*Finance Minister.*	*Surplus.*	*Deficit.*
		£	£
1864-5	Sir Charles Trevelyan	—	193,520
1865-6	Sir Charles Trevelyan	2,800,491	—
1866-7	Mr. W. N. Massey	—	2,517,491
1867-8	Mr. W. N. Massey	—	1,610,157
1868-9	Sir Richard Temple	—	4,144,643
5 Years		2,800,491	8,465,811
Actual Deficit			5,665.320
Public Works Extraordinary			1,973,075
Net Deficit			3,692,245

last three years of his office nearly three millions sterling were spent on large irrigation works.

Next in importance to canals came the development of railways and the completion of the trunk lines projected by Lord Dalhousie. India can always grow more than sufficient food for its population. In famine time the question is its distribution. Surplus food is of no use if it cannot be carried to markets of demand. Railways and good country roads are perhaps even of more value in general famine than canals. They create in ordinary times an interchange of commodities and a coming and going of traffic which responds to the slightest call. In devising his railway projects, as in working out the scheme of canals, Lawrence had the benefit of the services of Colonel Richard Strachey. But these schemes were framed at the close of his Viceroyalty and were left to Lord Mayo to carry out. In Sir John Lawrence's time, however, £26,000,000 were spent on railways, the capital for construction rising from £55,000,000 to £81,000,000. Notwithstanding this, so rapid was the development of traffic that the net amount of interest on the capital (i. e. after deducting traffic receipts less working expenses), which was £1,700,000 in 1863–4, was only £1,203,000 in 1868. In the interval traffic earnings rose from £1,720,900 to £4,875,000.

It is to our English financiers we owe the system of decentralisation which has worked beneficial changes in Indian administration, and it was in

Lawrence's time that the scheme was first effectively discussed. Under the East India Company the financial relations between the Supreme and Local Governments were very much those of a merchant to his clerk. Everything was dependent on Calcutta, and there was no principle on which the assignments of money to subordinate Governments were regulated. Local Governments tried to get all they could, and, as is usual, the most clamorous, not necessarily the most necessitous or the most deserving, often got the biggest share. Those who had grown up under the system did not feel its inconvenience much; but the detail and the pitch-and-toss way of doing things were intolerable to administrators from England educated in the ways of self-government. Samuel Laing complained that the time of the Government of India, which should have been devoted to large and important matters, was frittered away in doing business which an experienced secretary would probably do better. Sir Henry Maine stigmatised it as 'parish vestry business,' and feared an inevitable collapse unless the strain were lightened. Lord Canning, by the creation of Provincial Legislatures, had given in one department of business the clue to the direction in which reform was to be looked for; and his Finance Minister, Mr. Laing, proposed to apply a similar remedy to the finances. He made a bold attempt to break through what he called 'the system of barren uniformity and pedantic centralisation which have tended in times past to reduce all India to dependence on the *bureaux* of Calcutta,' and to give to Local Governments the power and the responsibility of managing their own local affairs.

His scheme was to transfer from imperial to provincial budgets charges amounting to £500,000 with power to raise the amount by local taxation. But the plan fell through, because it was not thought fair to anticipate the action of the Local Legislatures which were then being established, in a matter so peculiarly within their province. Sir Charles Trevelyan approved of the principle, but took no active steps to deal with it as a whole. The scheme, however, was revived by Mr. Massey. He proposed to transfer to local account charges amounting in all to £1,200,000, to be raised by local taxation. Local Governments would gladly have accepted the charges had they been provided with the means of meeting them, but took fright at the taxation. So the scheme was modified to the transfer of charges together with assignments of revenue sufficient to meet them on the existing scale of expenditure, any future increase of outlay under the assigned heads being met from the growth of local revenue or economy under some other local head of charge. General Richard Strachey was employed to work out the details on the figures of Mr. Massey's budget; and the scheme, which was favourably viewed by the Local Governments, became the basis of the measures afterwards adopted by Lord Mayo.

Personally Sir John Lawrence was not much inclined to the plan. He believed that financial control could be made effective by simpler measures. He did not like to interfere with arrangements which had been introduced by Mr. James Wilson only a few years before. And he was afraid that the relaxation of centralised control would end in extravagance, waste of resources, and ultimate taxation, of which he had a sincere horror. But he allowed the scheme to be fully worked out, and it was one of the important matters of business which he advised Lord Mayo to carefully study before he left for India. This excellent measure, which Lord Mayo worked out, revolutionised the financial administration. But as first introduced it had many defects. The assignments were based upon actual expenditure at the time; so that the Governments that had been most extravagant, and therefore presumably not most deserving, got most benefit. The heads assigned—jails, police, printing, roads, and so forth—were spending-heads, and only to a very limited extent revenue-producing; so that material improvement in income was hardly to be expected, even with careful management. Provinces that had long been under British rule and had got their wants fairly supplied out of the general revenues were well off; backward and new provinces, poorly provided with public buildings, jails, colleges and hospitals, found themselves in difficulties. Some got more than they could profitably spend; while others were hampered in their progress.

It was in a few years found necessary, in place of a fixed grant, to give a fixed share in the land-revenue and other expanding sources of income. With the adoption of this principle all the provinces at once entered on a career of progress and rapid development. The provincial resources at the disposal of Local Governments in the year 1889–90 amounted to the large sum of £19,500,000. While decentralisation has led to development of revenues and economy in expenditure on the part of Local Governments, it has not been without effect in checking imperial extravagance. The Government of India has to be sure of its ground before laying its hand upon the provincial revenues or balances. 'I can quite conceive,' said Sir Henry Maine[1], 'a campaign on the Oxus or the Jaxartes being undertaken with less precipitation, if the Supreme Government had lost the power of summarily stopping all public works throughout India, and could only pay for military glory by borrowing or taxation!' One of the greatest advantages, however, is that it has put an end to the craze for pedantic uniformity of administration, and led to that variety of expedient which is essential to the proper government of a country so large as India, with diversities of climate, conditions and possibilities, and with a population in every stage of advancement from that of almost naked savages to a culture not surpassed in any of the cities of Europe.

[1] Minute dated September 13, 1867.

Another of the problems with which Sir John Lawrence had to deal was the commencement of that fluctuation in the ratio of the value of gold to silver which has played such havoc in the exchange between India and countries possessing a gold currency. The difficulty began to be felt in the cotton speculations. The desire for a gold currency, however, had previously manifested itself among the English merchants. As a tentative step towards the adoption of a gold standard, the Government decided to receive and issue sovereigns at the rate of ten rupees and to accept them in the Currency Office to the extent of one-fourth of the notes represented by coin and bullion. In this way it was hoped that the demand in the country for a gold currency would be tested. But the sovereigns were not made a legal tender, and the experiment was doomed to failure. Gold began to rise in value as measured by silver in the ordinary market, and the treasury price had to be raised. But this had no effect. Obviously, as the Currency Commission reported in 1866, it was necessary either to give the experiment up altogether or to do a great deal more. Either some means would have to be devised to fix the ratio of gold to silver, or silver coins would have to be reduced to tokens for the payment of small sums and silver demonetised in favour of a gold currency.

Whatever opinions may be held as to the practicability of a double standard, it is certain that the two metals cannot run together as coinage at fluctuating values; and that India could not by herself stereotype in silver the value of gold. If it be possible to fix a ratio of value between the precious metals, such a measure can only be effected by a common understanding among the principal countries of the world; but from that condition we seem to be almost as far off now as then. On the other hand to demonetise silver in India was at that time impossible. Sufficient gold did not exist in the country. The disturbance to the revenue settlements and to obligations contracted in silver was deemed prohibitive. Gold was accordingly left to rise and fall in relation to silver like any other commodity; and the experiment failed. But it was a courageous attempt to grapple with a difficult problem, and to feel the way towards a solution of what has grown to be the largest financial question with which India has to deal.

This is not the place to discuss the problem whether, upon the whole, India has lost or gained by her fidelity to silver as her standard of value. The change in the gold value of silver from the long customary par of 60*d.* the oz. or four ounces to the pound sterling, to 40*d.* an oz. or six ounces to the pound sterling, increases the burden of the fixed gold charges of India from 140 to 210 millions of rupees—i.e. by 70 millions of rupees, equal to £4,500,000—a phenomenon which necessarily produces constant financial anxiety. Nor can we predict the exact point at which the further depreciation of silver will be arrested. Nevertheless, India has not sunk under the burden; indeed she has never been more prosperous financially than now; so that there may be compensations which, though not so obvious as this great loss, counteract and outweigh it. My present object is to show that the importance of the question was recognised by Sir John Lawrence on its earliest appearance. It was not till much later that it attained its full development.

CHAPTER XI

Foreign Affairs. Afghánistán

The temptation is strong to give a general review of Sir John Lawrence's dealings with the independent Oriental powers with whom the Government of India has diplomatic relations. The subject possesses some interest, but space forbids. I select for notice only the affairs of Afghánistán. They are of more interest than the rest; they directly touch the foundations of our Indian Empire; they have brought Indian affairs within the range of European diplomacy; and Lawrence's attitude towards them has been both misunderstood and misrepresented. I do not purpose to linger over their early history—the treaties of friendship with Dost Muhammad in 1855 and 1857; the attitude of Afghánistán during the mutiny; Sir John's proposal, first made when the Delhi cloud lowered blackest, to abandon Peshâwar to Dost Muhammad and concentrate our forces on Lahore and Múltán. These and other matters of the kind are only of passing interest. It is not until the projected shadow of Russia fell upon the States on the North of Afghánistán that Kábul affairs begin to assume permanent importance.

Seven months before Sir John Lawrence returned to India as Viceroy, his old friend Dost Muhammad died, at a great age. He had just captured Herát after a long siege, and reduced all the provinces of Afghánistán to his sway. He left sixteen sons. His death was the signal for family dissensions which rent his Kingdom asunder. The story is a tangled skein of treachery and bloodshed. I will try to unravel only so much of it as is needful for a judgment on Lawrence's policy. Its main bearings can be sufficiently understood if all the actors are discarded except the following five:—(1) Sher Alí, the third son of Dost Muhammad; (2) and (3) his two elder half-brothers, Afzal, Governor of Turkestán in the North; and Ázim, Governor of Kuram in the East; (4) his younger, uterine brother Amín, Governor of Kandahár; and (5) Abdúl Rahmán, son of Afzal and now reigning Amír of Afghánistán.

Sher Alí was the heir designate, and had been recognised as such by Lord Canning. He ascended the throne in accordance with his father's choice. The Amír was greatly pleased with the appointment of Lawrence, whom he could claim as a friend of former days. In March, 1864, Sher Alí despatched an Envoy to him with letters, in which he asked for a renewal of the treaty made with his father, the gift of 6000 muskets, and the recognition of his son, Muhammad Alí, as Heir Apparent. On the 4th of May Sir John Lawrence replied, intimating that the old treaty was still in force, recognising Muhammad Alí, but refusing the gift of arms. Meanwhile insurrection, which had been smouldering all winter, broke out in spring. The two brothers Afzal and Ázim began to assert their independence in April. Ázim was easily defeated, and driven to seek refuge in British territory. Afzal, in the North, who had proclaimed himself Amír, and made alliance with the King of Bokhára, was a more formidable rival. But after an indecisive battle a peace was patched up. Sher Alí swore friendship on the Korán, and the brothers made a tour of the province of Turkestán together. The reconciliation, however, was hollow. Suddenly Sher Alí put his brother Afzal in irons, and carried him back a captive to Kábul. Abdúl Rahmán fled to Bokhára. This treachery caused great excitement and seriously shook Sher Alí's power. The winter of 1864 settled down gloomily in Kábul, with forebodings of disaster and the certainty of fresh troubles in the spring.

Early in 1865 Ázim left British territory and wandered in the Wazírí Hills biding his time. Sher Alí was informed, and expressed his thanks for the warning. Meanwhile Amín, in Kandahár, tried to persuade the British Government to recognise his independence. But Sir John Lawrence told him that our 'treaty relations were with the Amír; and the British Government could not consent to recognise in any way the independence of any of his relations, or give any countenance to proceedings having for their object the assertion and establishment of such independence.' Of these communications Sher Alí was again duly informed. In May the Amír set out to reduce his brother to obedience, and wrote to tell the Viceroy; who replied, regretting the divisions in the Bárakzai family and hoping 'that the Ruler of all things would so order the course of events that a compromise might be effected among his Highness' relations which would conduce to the prosperity of his country and the consolidation of his power.' The result of the campaign was the defeat of the Kandahár forces at Kujhbáz on the 6th of June. In the thick of the battle, Amín and Muhammad Alí met face to face and engaged in single combat. Uncle and nephew were both slain. Sher Alí entered Kandahár in triumph, but the loss of his son dimmed the victory. His bereavement clouded his reason; he became morose to his courtiers, disgraced his best general, and gave way to extravagance of grief. For nine months this madness lasted; and in the interval events happened in the North which cost him the throne of Kábul.

Abdúl Rahmán, having got help from the King of Bokhára, crossed the Oxus and marched on Kábul to release his captive father. Ázim joined him on the way. By the spring of 1866, the confederates had made themselves masters of the capital of Afghánistán. Throughout Turkestán prayers were said in the name of the King of Bokhára; in Kábul they were offered for 'the Ruler of the day.' At this juncture the British Agent offered compliments to Ázim, for which he was rebuked by his Government. So long, it was said, as Sher Alí retained any material hold in

Afghánistán, the Government of India intended to continue to him its recognition unimpaired. Ázim now wrote reporting his successes, and received an answer in general terms of courtesy. At this time Lawrence defined his policy in the following terms:—'We should not be hasty in giving up the Amír's cause as lost. We should await the development of events, and for the present continue to recognise Sher Alí as the Amír of Afghánistán. If the Amír fail in his attempt to recover Kábul, and Sardár Muhammad Ázim Khán establish his power and make overtures to the British Government, the latter can then be recognised as the ruler of such parts of the country as he may possess. It should be our policy to show clearly that we will not interfere in the struggle; that we will not aid either party; that we will leave the Afgháns to settle their own quarrels; and that we are willing to be on terms of amity and good-will with the nation and with their rulers *de facto*.'

At last the successes of his enemies roused Sher Alí from his lethargy, and he put himself at the head of his troops. Dissensions ran high at Kábul. The country between the capital and Kandahár was a sea of anarchy. Sher Alí's prospects were good. The Kábul troops retreated as he advanced, and Ázim's cause seemed doomed. On the 10th of May, 1866, the armies met in battle at Sheikhábád. Fortune was inclining to the Amír, and it seemed as if he would win the day, when, all at once, the Kandahár regiments went over to the enemy, and Sher Alí's cause was lost.

The Amír fled wounded from the field. Ghazní shut its gates in his face, and he found no resting-place till he reached Kandahár. All his camp and munitions of war were taken; the captive Afzal was released and proclaimed Amír; Kábul was illuminated; kettledrums were beaten at the gates; and coins were struck in Afzal's name. Kandahár and Herát were all that remained to Sher Alí of his father's kingdom. The British Agent was now permitted to present himself before Afzal as the ruler of Kábul.

On May 30, Afzal wrote to the Viceroy reviewing the events of the last two years, and hoping that the relations of friendship which subsisted with Dost Muhammad might be maintained with him. He received an answer, dated July 11, and addressed to him as Walí of Kábul, in which Sir John Lawrence expressed sincere sorrow for the misfortunes which had befallen the great House of the Bárakzais and the calamities, so heavy and protracted, which had been suffered by the people. 'While I am desirous,' he said, 'that the alliance between the two Governments should be firm and lasting, it is incumbent on me to tell Your Highness that it would be inconsistent with the fame and reputation of the British Government to break off its alliance with Amír Sher Alí Khán, who has given it no offence, so long as he retains his authority and power over a large portion of Afghánistán. That Amír still rules in Kandahár and in Herát. My friend! the relations of this Government are with the actual rulers of Afghánistán. If Your Highness is able to consolidate Your Highness' power in Kábul, and is sincerely desirous of being a friend and ally of the British Government, I shall be ready to accept Your Highness as such. But I cannot break the existing engagement with Amír Sher Alí Khán, and I must continue to treat him as the ruler of that portion of Afghánistán over which he retains control. Sincerity and fair dealing induce me to write this plainly and openly to Your Highness.'

Gathering his forces together, Sher Alí made another stroke for his throne. But he was disastrously defeated by Ázim and Abdúl Rahmán on January 17, 1867. Once more he fled from the field of battle. This time Kandahár shut its gates upon him, as Ghazní had done before, and he continued his flight to Herát. Afzal at once announced this victory to the Government of India. He was addressed in reply as ruler of Kábul and Kandahár. Sir John Lawrence, in his letter, expressed great pity for Sher Alí personally and concern for the welfare of the Bárakzai House and the Afghán people. He hailed hopefully any event that might tend to bring Afghánistán to stable peace and strong Government under one of the sons of Dost Muhammad. He said frankly that he had left them to fight out the battle on their own resources and would still do so if hostilities should unhappily be renewed; and that, so long as Sher Alí held Herát, he would recognise him as ruler of Herát and reciprocate his amity. 'But upon the same principle,' he added, 'I am prepared to recognise Your Highness as Amír of Kábul and Kandahár, and I frankly offer Your Highness in that capacity peace and the good-will of the British Government.'

A new development was given at this time to the policy of the Government of India by the proceedings of Sher Alí himself. Bent upon the recovery of the sovereignty of Afghánistán, he applied for help; and, when the correspondence with Afzal was explained to him, he showed an inclination to seek from Persia and Russia the assistance he had failed to get from us. The invocation of a foreign power entirely altered the case. Sir John Lawrence therefore suggested that if Sher Alí should take such a course, it would be for the interests of British India openly to assist the party in power at Kábul, with a moderate subsidy and a supply of arms, *to resist Sher Alí*. 'Our relations,' he said, 'should always be with the *de facto* ruler of the day; and so long as the *de facto* ruler is not unfriendly to us, we should always be prepared to renew with him the same terms as obtained under his predecessor.' Having regard also to the rapid advance of Russia in Central Asia, Lawrence suggested that some understanding should be come to with the Czar's Government, so that up to a certain point the relations of the British and Russian Governments should 'be openly acknowledged, and admitted as bringing them into necessary contact and treaty with the tribes and nations on the several sides of such a line. If an understanding, or even an engagement, of this nature were come to, the Government of India on the one hand could look on without anxiety or apprehension at the proceedings of Russia on her southern frontier, and welcome the civilising effect of her border Government on the wild tribes of the Steppe and on the bigoted and exclusive Governments of Bokhára and Khokand; while Russia, on the other hand, assured of our loyal feeling in this matter, would have no jealousy in respect of our alliance with the Afghán and neighbouring tribes, or of our negotiations to repress Persia in her designs upon the tracts which border upon her eastern frontier.'

Now it is important to bear in mind the time at which these suggestions were made. It was in September 1867. Russia had just annexed half of Khokand and reduced the other half to the position of a dependent State. She was only beginning those bold and rapid advances by which she has since lapped in her embrace the whole of the northern and western frontiers of Afghánistán. It is well known how, as she gradually recovered from the crushing disaster of the Crimean War, Russia set herself to make strong her position in Central Asia. This she did in two ways—first, by closing the open frontier between her advanced positions at Perovsk on the Orenberg line and Vernoe on the line of Siberia; and, secondly, by activity on the Caspian Sea, the occupation of Krasnovodsk and the advance along the Atrek. The second course was a later development, beginning in 1869 at the end of Lawrence's reign. The closing of the open frontier took place in 1864. Auliáta was taken by a force moving westward from Vernoe, the town of Turkestán by a force moving eastward from Perovsk, and the two detachments completed the line by occupying Chamkand in the centre. Thus Russia brought herself face to face with the three Usbeg Khánates of Khokand, Bokhára and Khíva. Their absorption in the Russian dominions was rapid.

Foreseeing their doom, the Khán of Khokand and the Amír of Bokhára endeavoured in vain to get help from Calcutta, Constantinople, and London. The Khokand Envoy was received at Lahore in October 1864, and was present at Sir John Lawrence's great Darbár there. He of Bokhára was received at Calcutta in January 1867. By this time the independence of both States had been destroyed. First of all, the Russian frontier was advanced to the Jaxartes by the occupation of Tashkand and Chináz in 1865. In the following year Khojand, Oratippa and Jizák were annexed, adding to the Russian territory 4,183 square miles south of the river. Bokhára fell next, by the occupation of Samarcand and Katikurgán and the absorption of 7,955 square miles of that Khánate. The Jaxartes had been crossed, but Samarcand had not yet been taken, at the time when Lawrence made the proposals I have quoted. When Samarcand fell, he pressed once more for some arrangement with Russia, and urged 'that it might be given to understand, in firm but courteous language, that it cannot be permitted to interfere in the affairs of Afghánistán or in those of any State which lies contiguous to our frontier.'

The proposals made by Sir John Lawrence at this early date—viz. assistance to the established Government of Kábul, and friendly negotiations with Russia—are alone sufficient to relieve him from the charge, so often brought against him, of indifference to the Russian advance. Out of these proposals grew all the subsequent policy—the grant of assistance to Sher Alí himself when he recovered the throne of Kábul, the great historical meeting with him at Ambálá in March 1869, the policy of a neutral zone between the Russian and the British spheres of influence in Central Asia, the negotiations with Russia for the delimitation of the northern and western frontiers of Afghánistán, and the measures taken for the consolidation of the Afghán Government down to the time of Lord Lytton.

The tedious story of the Bárakzai quarrels is now near its end. Suffice it to say that the star of Sher Alí suffered only a temporary eclipse. Afzal died after a lingering illness on 7th October, 1867. His brother Ázim ascended the throne and was formally recognised by the British Government. The rule of both brothers was detested. They were reigns of terror, of forced loans, of confiscations, of savage executions. Sher Alí, recovering his strength at Herát and aided by his friends in Turkestán, advanced on Kandahár, defeated the Kábul army, and pushing on to Kábul recovered his capital. Ázim's army melted away like snow in summer. He fled to Turkestán, where he and Abdúl Rahmán kept up a show of resistance for some months. In January 1869, however, they were completely crushed. Ázim fled to Persia, where he soon after died. His nephew found refuge in Bokhára, to emerge from obscurity ten years later as Amír of Afghánistán. Sher Alí was once more seated on the throne, undisputed ruler over all the possessions of his father Dost Muhammad.

As soon as he had recovered Kábul, Sher Alí wrote to the Governor-General to inform him; and received an answer congratulating him on the success due alone to his own courage, ability and firmness, and begging him to deal leniently with those who had fought against him. 'I am prepared,' said Sir John Lawrence, 'not only to maintain the bonds of amity and good-will which were established between Amír Dost Muhammed Khán and myself, acting on behalf of the British Government, but so far as may be practicable to strengthen these bonds.' To Lawrence it had always been a cause of sorrow that the family of the great Dost had been broken up into contending factions, causing the ruin of many brave Chiefs and the general weakening of the Afghán power. He had made no secret of his regrets, and had done his best to encourage the brothers to be reconciled, though he would not interfere to strengthen one against the other. Now at last there seemed a prospect of a consolidated power. Sher Alí had not only recovered his throne and beaten down all his enemies, but he had been welcomed back to Kábul by the very soldiers and people who had deserted him. The time seemed to have now come when, without wrong to any one and without committing the Government to a course of interference in Afghánistán, it was possible to strengthen the Amír, to restore peace in the distracted and ruined country, to secure the Amír's good-will, and at the same time to maintain a friendly power between India and the Russian possessions in Central Asia. 'While strictly refusing to enter into anything like an offensive and defensive alliance with the Amír of Kábul,' he said, 'I think it should be carefully explained to him that we are interested in the security of his dominions from foreign invasion, and that, provided he remains strictly faithful to his engagements, we are prepared to support his independence; but that the manner of doing so must rest with ourselves.'

In pursuance of this policy Sir John Lawrence sent the Amír a present of £60,000 and 3,500 stand of arms. The Secretary of State gave him *carte blanche.* 'Act on your own judgment in assisting Amír Sher Alí in the manner proposed.' Sher Alí was very grateful. He was preparing to go to India to meet Sir John Lawrence when troubles in Turkestán detained him. He could not leave till he had put down his enemies; and this was not effected till the beginning of 1869. Meanwhile Lawrence's Viceroyalty was drawing to a close. Three days before handing over his high office, he wrote the Amír a farewell letter promising the gift of £60,000 more 'as a further proof of the desire of the British Government, which fears no aggression and which wishes for no conquest, to see a strong, a just and a merciful Government established by Your Highness at Kábul and throughout Afghánistán.' He asked for no other return from the Amír than abiding confidence, sincerity and goodwill, and he held out hopes of future help in money or materials of war as the Government of India might year by year see fit. This policy Lawrence maintained to be no change, but in perfect accordance with the course hitherto followed, and to be justified by the events which had replaced Sher Alí on the throne. It commanded the assent and approval of Her Majesty the Queen. The Amír was assured that, so long as he continued by his actions to evince a real desire for the alliance of the British Government, he had nothing to apprehend in the way of a change of policy or of our interference in the internal affairs and administration of his Kingdom.

Having put down all his enemies in the North, Sher Alí was at length free to visit India. On January 18, 1869, he wrote to the Viceroy reporting his successes, and sent a message through the British Agent renewing his request for an interview. By this time Sir John Lawrence had left the country. The interview, as every one knows, was the historical meeting with Lord Mayo at Ambálá on March 27, 1869, at which, as the Russian newspapers said at the time, 'the first stone of the wall was laid which the Anglo-Indian Government is hastening to build across the path of the Russians in Central Asia.'

It has been said that to leave the contending factions, as Lawrence did, to fight out their quarrels, and to recognise the *de facto* ruler, was to invite competition for the throne. But as a matter of fact, the competition for the throne began when Sher Alí was the recognised Amír and his son was the recognised Heir Apparent. The attempt of Amín to throw off his allegiance was discountenanced and condemned. The British Agent was rebuked for his premature acknowledgment of Ázim. It was not till Sher Alí was a fugitive and his cause seemed hopelessly lost, that Sir John Lawrence recognised any other than himself. It was not till Afzal's power seemed firmly established in Kábul that he was recognised as ruler of so much of the country as he had conquered. As a matter of fact, the provinces of Afghánistán were generally held on what was practically an independent tenure, and only a strong ruler, like Dost Muhammad, had succeeded in uniting them into one Kingdom.

The question of when it is right or prudent to recognise a *de facto* Government must depend on the circumstances of each case. Moral recognition with a denial of material support can be of little value in the contest for a throne like that of Afghánistán, to which there was no recognised law of rightful succession. Our recognition of Sher Alí did not prevent him from losing his Kingdom; nor did our recognition of Ázim enable him to maintain the throne of Kábul. So far as moral influence could go, Lawrence used it to reconcile the family quarrel. To have interfered, with material help, to maintain upon the throne a ruler not acknowledged by his people, was a dangerous policy forbidden by the provisions of existing treaties. Our experience of its evil fruits was recent and bitter. This much, at any rate, is certain—that the policy which Lawrence pursued met with general acceptance at the time. Lord Mayo's policy was no reversal, but a continuation and development of it.

No one admitted this more frankly than Lord Mayo himself. No one was more impressed than he with the necessity of abstaining from interference in Afghánistán. He would have no European Officers placed as Residents in the cities; no offensive and defensive treaty. Under no circumstances would he send a British soldier across the frontier to coerce the Amír's rebellious subjects. He would, almost using Lawrence's own words, 'let them know that if they chose to quarrel, they must fight it out without any assistance from us.' His promise to the Amír to 'view with severe displeasure any attempts on the part of his rivals to disturb his position as ruler of Kábul and rekindle civil war,' was carefully explained as being limited to moral means, and went little, if at all, beyond what Sir John Lawrence actually did. In regard to pecuniary assistance to Sher Alí, Lord Mayo did not even go so far as Lawrence. He gave at Ambálá only the second sum of £60,000 which

Lawrence had promised, but held out no hope of a yearly subsidy. In all essential respects his policy was a continuance of that of his predecessor. 'I believe,' he said in a letter to Lord Lawrence himself, 'that when you sent Sher Alí the money and arms last December, you laid the foundation of a policy which will be of the greatest use to us hereafter. I wish to continue it.' The Government of India, too, was careful to explain that one of the good results of the interview with Sher Alí was that 'it has assured His Highness that the policy which was adopted by His Lordship's predecessor, on the Amír's regaining the throne of Kábul in August last, will be continued.' Lord Clarendon also took some pains to assure Prince Gortschakoff, when he met him at Heidelberg in the autumn of 1869, that the policy of the Indian Government towards Sher Alí was not of recent date, and had originated with Lord Lawrence.

There came indeed a time, nearly a decade later, when the policy was reversed; when it was determined to interfere in Afghánistán; when it was resolved to force a Resident upon the Amír; when Afghánistán was even dismembered, and a separate ruler was set up in Kandahár. The new policy ended in disaster, and, after the destruction of the Afghán Government in a war which no one now-a-days ventures to justify, the work of consolidation had to be begun anew. I need not here discuss the question of the so-called scientific frontier, or enquire whether the treasure which has been sunk in fortifications far in advance of our old frontier might not have been more usefully spent. Doubtless the frontier towards Kandahár is now impregnable. Many, however, think it was so before, and that the defences which nature has provided in barren rocks, a waterless desert, and inhospitable tribes, are stronger than those of our military engineers. I am not competent to form a judgment on the military question, but of this I am sure—that, considering the conditions of our tenure in India, no forward policy can hope to be successful if it is not supplemented by what was the essence of the policy of Lawrence—the contentment of the masses of the people. If in India we were all of one blood and language and religion, the question of frontier defence might be left to be decided on military and financial considerations alone. But there is a social and a moral element which we dare not ignore. Our dominion is that of a foreign people, few in numbers and with a European army so limited that the concentration of it on an advanced frontier necessarily weakens our hold on the rear. If at the same time our moral hold be weak and our power be not 'broad based' upon the contentment of the people, a disaster in the front may shake the Empire to its foundations. It was in this conviction that Sir John Lawrence's Government explained its policy in language which cannot be improved upon:—

'Should a foreign power, such as Russia, ever seriously think of invading India from without or, what is more probable, of stirring up the elements of disaffection or anarchy within it, our true policy, our strongest security, would then, we conceive, be found to lie in previous abstinence from entanglements at either Kábul, Kandahár, or any similar outpost; in full reliance on a compact, highly equipped and disciplined army, stationed within our own territories or on our own border; in the contentment if not in the attachment of the masses; in the sense of security of title and possession with which our whole policy is gradually imbuing the minds of the principal Chiefs and the Native aristocracy; in the construction of material works within British India which enhance the comfort of the people, while they add to our political and military strength; in husbanding our finances and consolidating and multiplying our resources; in quiet preparation for all contingencies which no Indian statesmen should disregard; and in a trust in the rectitude and honesty of our intentions, coupled with the avoidance of all sources of complaint which either invite foreign aggression or stir up restless spirits to domestic revolt.'

The wisdom of these views is not to be questioned.

CHAPTER XII

The End

The end had now come, and Sir John Lawrence was to put off his armour, battered and dented in many a conflict. 'It was a proud moment to me,' he said in a conversation with his son-in-law, which is touchingly recorded by Bosworth Smith, 'when I walked up the steps of this house feeling as I then did that, without political interest or influence, I had been chosen to fill the highest office under the Crown, the Viceroyalty of the Queen. But it will be a happier moment to me when I walk down the steps with the feeling that I have tried to do my duty.' Lord Mayo arrived on the 12th of January, 1869. From that day a new Viceroy reigned. A public banquet had been given to Sir John Lawrence the night before in the town-hall of Calcutta. He took the opportunity to defend his foreign policy, which had been assailed. Like his great master Dalhousie, he was sensitive to the criticisms of the local Press, which, with one or two honourable exceptions, had not the high sense of responsibility twenty years ago that it has since acquired. He over-estimated its influence

N 2

and had often been wounded by its prejudiced and ill-informed comments. As he now took farewell of his countrymen he spoke with visible emotion. His last words were to beg them 'to be just and kind to the Natives of India.' On the 19th of January he left the shores of India for ever. Further honours awaited him in his native country. He was raised to the peerage under the title of Baron Lawrence of the Punjab and Grateley, and his annuity of £2000 a year was extended for the life of his immediate successor.

Lord Lawrence bore his fresh honours modestly. All through his public career he was the plain Englishman, as simple in his ways when he was Viceroy as when he was a District Magistrate. The Chief Commissioner would travel on the mail-cart like any junior Officer. The Governor-General would walk to church and dispense with sentries and escorts, to the consternation of his staff. 'I never cared for,' he remarked when laying down the Viceroyalty, 'and I do not regret the resignation of, all the state, pomp, power, or patronage which appertain to the office.' Perhaps he was too indifferent to the value of pomp and circumstance in the East, though in his great Darbárs at Lahore and Agra, in dealing with the warrior Chiefs of the Punjab or the chivalry of Rájaputána, he maintained a dignity and state not inferior to the most kingly of Viceroys. But the simplicity of his ways exposed him to the poisoned shafts of malice and to misrepresentations which pained him.

Nor had every one eyes to see the true nobility that was in him, and how he was,

> 'As the greatest only are,
> In his simplicity sublime.'

His power of work was immense. No old bullock, he remarked, is worked harder. 'I have all my life been a hard worker,' he said, 'and it has now become a second nature to me. I work therefore as much from habit as from principle.' His aim was to do the day's work within the day if he could. Certain things had to be done; there was a certain time to do them in; and he held that a good administrator would distribute his time so as to do them all. In the autumn of 1858, my office was in a small room adjoining one in which he occasionally worked when at Lahore. I often saw him at his table. He used to sit at his desk with a Native clerk squatted on the floor on each side of him and dictated to them his orders in short, swift sentences, as they alternately read aloud to him the vernacular documents.

His English correspondence was disposed of, for the most part, by brief notes on the margin of the letters for the guidance of his secretaries. It was an excellent method in the Punjab, where he was familiar with every question that came before him and knew its history from the beginning. But it was not so suitable in the Government of India, where cases had sometimes a history running back for fifty or a hundred years, generally through several Viceroyalties, occasionally with a shifting policy, and when now and then the 'previous correspondence' measured a foot or two thick! He tried it to begin with, but was soon glad to revert to the system of historical notes, in which a summary was given for his information. In the notes however he always required brevity and only the kernel of the case, with references to letters which he could read for himself if he wanted the details. 'Nobody will read your paper,' he said to one of his secretaries, pointing to a long memorandum on a subject which was attracting public attention. 'All the world will read that!' he added, as he handed to the secretary his own brief paragraph, which contained his statement of the question and his decision on it.

A rugged exterior and blunt manner covered the kindliest of hearts. 'I would give you the same advice if you were my own son,' he once said to me, after he had taken infinite pains in a personal matter about which I had consulted him. People might wince under his abrupt touch as he laid his finger on a fault; but he was a poor creature who took offence or fell away from his devotion to him on that account. He would often heal the smart of his rebuke by a kindly joke. For he held with Horace and with Milton, that

> 'Joking decides great things;
> Stronger and better oft than earnest can.'

He had his enemies like other men—some of them

bitter ones. But the honesty, the truthfulness, the guileless candour of the man were so transparent that, as Lord Stanley said, 'malice itself has never fastened upon Lord Lawrence's career the imputation of one discreditable incident or one unworthy act.'

In the autumn of 1870, Lord Lawrence allowed himself to be nominated for election to the London School Board, under the Elementary Education Act which had just come into force. It was not work for which he was naturally suited. He hated Boards, and considered himself constitutionally ill-fitted, as we have seen, to be member even of a Council of Three. He was no speaker, and the practical training of an Indian career, in which there is much writing and little talk, was not such as to cultivate the gifts required for the conduct of affairs in a large Board of fluent debaters. He had governed an Empire; and his acceptance of the seemingly humble position on the School Board was only an illustration of the principle he had acted out all his life—that no work was too insignificant to be done by his own hand, and that it was simply his duty to do the work that lay before him in the sphere to which his Lord and Master was pleased to call him. For three years he acted as Chairman of the Board, with the diligence that was to be expected and with acceptance to his colleagues. His term of office came to an end in November, 1873, and he declined to stand again on account of failing health. A cloud that had hung over his life now began to settle down upon him.

When a boy he had an attack of ophthalmia which, it is to be feared, permanently affected his eyes. The glare of the burning sun on the dry plains of Upper India, and the daily perusal of Oriental manuscripts, did not tend to improve them. Early in his career he had to beg his friends not to cross their letters, as he was almost blind with reading manuscripts. 'I fear if I live to fifty,' he once wrote, 'I shall be blind.' In 1876 his eyesight began to fail him altogether. 'The difficulty which my husband had in reading the morning prayers,' says Lady Lawrence in a memorandum quoted at length by Bosworth Smith, 'first opened our eyes; for he was often obliged to hand over the book to me.' An operation had to be undergone. It proved a failure. It was followed by terrible agony and weeks of blindness and pain, 'borne with the most wonderful sweetness and patience, as day followed day of ever-increasing suffering.' Eventually it was found that the sight of one eye was entirely gone and the other so weakened that it could not endure strong light. The anticipation of blindness was terrible to him. A second operation had to be undergone in March 1877 to remove the cataract, and again a slight 'needle-operation' in July. The eyesight was saved, but he was never again able to read or write and could not go about alone. The 'drop serene' or 'dim suffusion veiled' fell not on him, as on Milton, ere half his days were spent, but in the evening and twilight of life. Indeed it may be said of him that he died in harness.

After giving up the London School Board, he continued to take an interest in the Church Missionary Society and other religious institutions. He attended their meetings and bore public testimony to the value of the work done by missionaries in India. 'I believe,' he said at a meeting of the Wesleyan Missionary Society, 'notwithstanding all that the English people have done to benefit that country, the missionaries have done more than all other agencies combined.' When he could no longer read or write, he dictated the well-known letters to the *Times* by which he helped to rouse the English people to a sense of the iniquity of the Afghán War into which we had plunged. Undeterred by misrepresentation and abuse, he laboured as Chairman of the Afghán Committee to get hostilities at all events postponed; and by his letters he sought to bring back the Ministry to the policy of non-interference in Afghánistán, and the peaceful consolidation of the Government of that country by friendly support, which had been pursued by himself and two succeeding Viceroys. He took an active share in work among the poor and in some of the charitable institutions of London. Only a short week before his death, he was at the anniversary festival of the Asylum at Hampstead for the orphan daughters of soldiers. And 'it is a touching circumstance,' says Cust, 'and worthy of record, that the Angel of Death came to him at a time when invitations were actually in circulation to friends to meet at his house to discuss the affairs of the Christian Vernacular Education Society.'

He made his last appearance in the House of Lords on the 19th of June 1879, when he took part in the debate on the Indian budget. He returned home exhausted. Some days before, he had caught a cold which settled on him. On the 27th of June he died. 'I am so weary.' These, his biographer tells us, were his last words as he entered into his rest.

'So passed the strong heroic soul away.'

His virtues compelled eulogium even from those who differed most from his views and who tried to undo his policy. A notification in the *Gazette of India*, from Lord Lytton's pen, and written with all his own aptitude, expressed the general feeling:—

'No statesman since Warren Hastings,' it said, 'has administered the Government of India with a genius and an experience so exclusively trained and developed in her service, as those of the illustrious man whose life, now closed in the fulness of fame though not of age, bequeaths to his country a bright example of all that is noblest in the high qualities for which the Civil Service of India has justly been renowned; and in which, with such examples before it, it will never be deficient. The eminent services rendered to India by Lord Lawrence, both as ruler of the Punjab in the heroic defence of British power, and as Viceroy in the peaceful administration of a rescued Empire, cannot be fitly acknowledged in this sad record of the grief which she suffers by his death, and of the pride with which she cherishes his name.'

A grateful country made his grave in Westminster Abbey among the heroes and the great men of England.

He lies close by his old friend Lord Clyde (Sir Colin Campbell), with Sir James Outram on his left—the motto on his tomb 'Be ready.' Three monuments—in London, Calcutta, and Lahore—express the gratitude of the nation. In his old room at Haileybury, a tablet bearing his name may still inspire ingenuous youth with the same simple faith, heroic endurance, and transparent honesty. His name and the story of Delhi will live in the memory of his country as long as the English language is spoken.

Note to Page 19.

The best authority on the subject is the *Genealogical Memoirs of John Knox and of the Family of Knox*, by the Rev. Charles Rogers, LL.D., printed for the Grampian Club, 1876.

Bosworth Smith says that Letitia Catherine Knox was descended from the Scotch Reformer. This is certainly incorrect. John Knox's two sons, Nathaniel and Eleazer, both died unmarried. Sir Herbert Edwardes, in his *Life of Sir*

Henry Lawrence, makes the connection through Bishop Andrew Knox of the Scottish House of Ranfurlie, whom he surmises to have been a grand-nephew of the Reformer. M'Crie, in his *Life of Knox*, quotes David Buchanan, Historian of the Reformation, as authority for the statement that Knox's 'father was a brother's son of the House of Ranfurlie.' On the other hand, there is evidence that the family of John Knox was settled in Haddington as far back as 1488, so that the relationship to the Ranfurlie stock must have been remote.

Andrew Knox was minister of Lochwinnoch, Ayrshire, in 1581, and afterwards (1585) of the Abbey Church of Paisley. He became Bishop of the Isles in 1606 and Bishop of Raphoe in 1611. He held both Sees till 1619, when he resigned that of the Isles. He died on March 27, 1633, at the age of 74. He seems to have been a self-willed and masterful man. It may be worth while to rescue the following notes of him from the mass of dry genealogical details.

It is related of him that in 1592, at the head of a party of students from the College of Glasgow, he discomfited an armed band who, in the service of the King of Spain, had landed on Ailsa Craig in the hope of re-establishing the Roman faith in Scotland. On December 16, 1597, an Act was passed by the Estates of Parliament whereby he was declared to have done 'loyell and gud seruice to His Majestie and his cuntrey.' In October, 1604, when minister of Paisley, it was ordered, as a punishment for a violent assault he had committed on a Solicitor, with whom he had a quarrel and whose head he cut open with an iron key, that 'he sall sit in the maist patent place of the Kirk of Paisley, vpone Sunday the 19th inst. : and . . . in all humiliation, sal confess his offence to God, his brethren and the pairtie offendit, and sall sit doun vpone his knees and ask God mercie for the same.' He carried away with him to Ireland the two best bells from the Priory of Ardchattan and Abbey of Icolmkill, which his successor in the bishopric of Raphoe was compelled, by royal edict dated March 14, 1635, to restore.

It is a pity the connection with this old granite character breaks down. But according to Crawford's *MSS. Genealogy* (in the Advocates' Library, Edinburgh), quoted by Rogers, and written about the year 1726, the male posterity of Bishop Andrew Knox had become extinct, though of his daughters there were many descendants.

According to Rogers, Letitia's father, Rev. George Knox, Rector of Lifford, and son of George Knox of Minnymore (otherwise Moneymore), in the county of Donegal, was of the family of the Knoxes of Prehen, in county Londonderry, which family is descended from the Scottish House of Ranfurlie.

INDEX

THE END.

RULERS OF INDIA

THE CLARENDON PRESS SERIES OF INDIAN HISTORICAL RETROSPECTS.

Edited by SIR W. W. HUNTER, K.C.S.I., M.A., LL.D.

The following 29 volumes have been already published:—

I. *A BRIEF HISTORY OF THE INDIAN PEOPLES*, by SIR WILLIAM WILSON HUNTER, K.C.S.I. New and Revised Edition, Eighty-ninth Thousand, by W. H. HUTTON, B.D. (1903). 3s. 6d.

II. *BÁBAR: the Founder of the Mughal Dynasty.* By STANLEY LANE-POOLE, Esq., M.A., Professor of Arabic, Trinity College, Dublin; Author of *The Life of Lord Stratford de Redcliffe.* 2s. 6d.

III. *AKBAR: and the Rise of the Mughal Empire*, by COLONEL MALLESON, C.S.I., Author of *A History of the Indian Mutiny; The History of Afghanistan.* 2s. 6d.

IV. *ALBUQUERQUE: and the Early Portuguese Settlements in India*, by H. MORSE STEPHENS, Esq., M.A., Balliol College, formerly Lecturer on Indian History at Cambridge, Author of *The French Revolution; The Story of Portugal, &c.* 2s. 6d.

V. *AURANGZÍB: and the Decay of the Mughal Empire*, by STANLEY LANE-POOLE, Esq., M.A., Author of *The Coins of the Mughal Emperors; The Life of Stratford Canning; Catalogue of Indian Coins in the British Museum, &c.* 2s. 6d.

VI. *MADHAVA RAO SINDHIA: and the Hindú Reconquest of India*, by H. G. KEENE, Esq., M.A., C.I.E., Author of *The Moghul Empire, &c.* 2s. 6d.

VII. *LORD CLIVE: and the Establishment of the English in India*, by COLONEL MALLESON, C.S.I. 2s. 6d.

VIII. *DUPLEIX: and the Struggle for India by the European Nations*, by COLONEL MALLESON, C.S.I., Author of *The History of the French in India, &c.* 2s. 6d.

IX. *WARREN HASTINGS: and the Founding of the British Administration*, by CAPTAIN L. J. TROTTER, Author of *India under Victoria, &c.* 2s. 6d.

X. *THE MARQUESS CORNWALLIS: and the Consolidation of British Rule*, by W. S. SETON-KARR, Esq., sometime Foreign Secretary to the Government of India, Author of *Selections from the Calcutta Gazettes*, 3 vols. (1784–1805). 2s. 6d.

XI. *HAIDAR ALÍ AND TIPÚ SULTÁN: and the Struggle with the Muhammadan Powers of the South*, by LEWIN BENTHAM BOWRING, Esq., C.S.I., sometime Private Secretary to the Viceroy (Lord Canning) and Chief Commissioner of Mysore, Author of *Eastern Experiences*. 2s. 6d.

XII. *THE MARQUESS WELLESLEY: and the Development of the Company into the Supreme Power in India*, by the Rev. W. H. HUTTON, B.D., Fellow and Tutor of St. John's College, Oxford. 2s. 6d.

XIII. *THE MARQUESS OF HASTINGS: and the Final Overthrow of the Maráthá Power*, by MAJOR ROSS OF BLADENSBURG, C.B., Coldstream Guards; F.R.G.S. 2s. 6d.

XIV. *MOUNTSTUART ELPHINSTONE: and the Making of South-Western India*, by J. S. COTTON, Esq., M.A., formerly Fellow of Queen's College, Oxford, Author of *The Decennial Statement of the Moral and Material Progress and Condition of India*, presented to Parliament (1885), &c. 2s. 6d.

XV. *SIR THOMAS MUNRO: and the British Settlement of the Madras Presidency*, by JOHN BRADSHAW, Esq., M.A., LL.D., late Inspector of Schools, Madras. 2s. 6d.

XVI. *EARL AMHERST: and the British Advance eastwards to Burma*, chiefly from unpublished papers of the Amherst family, by Mrs. ANNE THACKERAY RITCHIE, Author of *Old Kensington, &c.*, and RICHARDSON EVANS, Esq. 2s. 6d.

XVII. *LORD WILLIAM BENTINCK: and the Company as a Governing and Non-trading Power*, by DEMETRIUS BOULGER, Esq., Author of *England and Russia in Central Asia; The History of China, &c.* 2s. 6d.

XVIII. *EARL OF AUCKLAND: and the First Afghan War*, by CAPTAIN L. J. TROTTER, Author of *India under Victoria, &c.* 2s. 6d.

XIX. *VISCOUNT HARDINGE: and the Advance of the British Dominions into the Punjab*, by his Son and Private Secretary, the Right Hon. VISCOUNT HARDINGE. 2s. 6d.

XX. *RANJIT SINGH: and the Sikh Barrier between our Growing Empire and Central Asia*, by SIR LEPEL GRIFFIN, K.C.S.I., Author of *The Punjab Chiefs, &c.* 2s. 6d.

XXI. *JOHN RUSSELL COLVIN: the last Lieutenant-Governor of the North-Western Provinces under the Company*, by his son, SIR AUCKLAND COLVIN, K.C.S.I., late Lieutenant-Governor of the North-Western Provinces. 2s. 6d.

XXII. *THE MARQUESS OF DALHOUSIE: and the Final Development of the Company's Rule*, by SIR WILLIAM WILSON HUNTER, K.C.S.I., M.A. 2s. 6d.

XXIII. *CLYDE AND STRATHNAIRN: and the Suppression of the Great Revolt*, by MAJOR-GENERAL SIR OWEN TUDOR BURNE, K.C.S.I., sometime Military Secretary to the Commander-in-Chief in India. 2s. 6d.

XXIV. *EARL CANNING: and the Transfer of India from the Company to the Crown*, by SIR HENRY S. CUNNINGHAM, K.C.I.E., M.A., Author of *British India and its Rulers, &c.* 2s. 6d.

XXV. *LORD LAWRENCE: and the Reconstruction of India under the Crown*, by SIR CHARLES UMPHERSTON AITCHISON, K.C.S.I., LL.D., formerly Foreign Secretary to the Government of India, and Lieutenant-Governor of the Punjab. 2s. 6d.

XXVI. *THE EARL OF MAYO: and the Consolidation of the Queen's Rule in India*, by SIR WILLIAM WILSON HUNTER, K.C.S.I., M.A., LL.D. 2s. 6d.

SUPPLEMENTARY VOLUMES.

XXVII. *JAMES THOMASON: and the British Settlement of North-Western India*, by SIR RICHARD TEMPLE, Bart., M.P., formerly Lieutenant-Governor of Bengal, and Governor of Bombay. 3s. 6d.

XXVIII. *ASOKA: The first Buddhist Emperor*, by VINCENT A. SMITH, M.R.A.S. 3s. 6d.

XXIX. *SIR HENRY LAWRENCE: The Pacificator*, by Lieut-General J. J. McLEOD INNES, R.E., V.C. 3s. 6d.